MARION MILNER was born in London in 1900. At the age of eleven she wanted to be a naturalist. At eighteen her interest turned from wild nature to human nature, and she began to train for work with very young children. She took a degree in psychology and physiology at London University. Following this, she worked in Industrial Psychology and then spent two years in the United States on a Rockefeller fellowship. *A Life of One's Own* was first published in 1934 and its companion volume, *An Experiment in Leisure*, in 1937. From 1934 to 1939 she did research work in girls' day schools in England and published her third book about it, *The Human Problem in Schools*, in 1938. She then trained as a psychoanalyst at the British Psychoanalytic Society. Her fourth book, *On Not Being Able to Paint* (1950), was based on a study of her own drawings and her fifth, *The Hands of the Living God* (1969, reprinted 1986), analyses the drawings of a patient with whom she worked for many years. Marion Milner is a Fellow of the British Psychological Society and her work is widely published in psycho-analytic journals. A collection of her papers will appear in 1987. She lives and works in Hampstead, London.

D1423713

A LIFE
OF
ONE'S OWN

Joanna Field
(Marion Milner)

—»»💿💿««—

Published by VIRAGO PRESS Limited 1986
41 William IV Street, London WC2N 4DB

This Virago edition is offset from the Pelican Books 1952
edition of this book, first published in 1934
by Chatto & Windus

Copyright Marion Milner 1934

British Library Cataloguing in Publication Data

Field, Joanna
A life of one's own.
1. Self-realization
Rn: Marion Milner I. Title
158.1   BF637.S4

ISBN 0-86068-821-6

Printed in Great Britain by Anchor Brendon Ltd
of Tiptree, Essex

To
D. M.

Acknowledgements

MY thanks are due to many, but particularly to Mary Dalston, Jan and Cora Gordon, S. G. H. Burger, and my husband, for continual help and encouragement; also to Dr Elton Mayo and Dr Irma Putnam for inspiration, though these last were not responsible for the use to which their wisdom was put and may even be embarrassed by this acknowledgement.

Contents

CONTENTS

Prefatory Note to the 1952 edition

A NEW EDITION, after sixteen years, of a book of such a personal nature as this raises certain problems. The deliberate endeavour to find a way of coming to terms with daily experience, which began in 1926, has continued during nearly twenty-five years of living. During this time the main issues have gradually become clearer; I have, however, made no substantial alteration in this book, except for certain minor omissions of those passages which now seem to me to be irrelevances and to confuse the main issue. The picture of the dragon has had to be left out because of cost of reproduction.

As for the Epilogue, I would not now describe the issues exactly in these terms, so I have made it much shorter, although not altered the main idea.

London

Preface

THIS book is the record of a seven years' study of living. The aim of the record was to find out what kinds of experience made me happy.

The method was: (*a*) to pick out those moments in my daily life which had been particularly happy and try to record them in words.

(*b*) To go over these records in order to see whether I could discover any rules about the conditions in which happiness occurred.

The form of the book follows from the nature of the experiment. I have tried to show the development of the problem by giving actual extracts from my diaries. I have tried always to keep to the facts as I saw them in order to show how I gradually pieced together the hints and clues which led to my final conclusions.

The reason for writing the book was not the same as the reason for publishing it. It was written in the spirit of a detective who, baffled by the multitude of his facts, goes over and makes a summary of the progress of his investigations in the hope of finding something he has missed. So, when I began to write this book, in the fourth year of my enterprise, I did not know, or could only perceive very dimly, what the end would be. In this sense the book is a contemporary journal of an exploration which involved doubts, delays, and expeditions on false trails, and the writing of it was an essential part of the search.

The reason for publishing the book is that although what I found is probably peculiar to my own temperament and circumstances, I think the method by which I found it may be useful to others, even to those whose discoveries about themselves may be the opposite of my own. The need for such a method in these days is obvious, a method for discovering one's true likes and dislikes, for finding and setting up a standard of values that is truly one's own and not a borrowed mass-produced ideal.

But although others besides myself may perhaps find the method useful, this book is in no sense a treatise on how to be happy. It is only as true a record as I could make it of what I myself found when I asked, 'What do I like?' It does not say, 'You must do this' – it only tries to give one answer to the question, 'What happens if you do this?' And since what did happen was a great surprise to me, I have no doubt that there will be others to whom the experiences described will also be remote and unfamiliar. For psychologists tell us that there are fundamental differences in temperament, the extreme of each kind completely misunderstanding and often despising its opposite. It also seems to be true that one can assume and strive after a false attitude, that is, an attitude contrary to the trend of one's nature; so there may perhaps be some who, if tempted to try the same experiment, may discover as I did myself that they are quite different creatures from what they had imagined.

Although there is this inevitable personal bias in my discoveries, there are some which I believe may apply universally. For instance, I discovered that there is all the difference in the world between knowing something intellectually and knowing it as a 'lived' experience. This is a truism but none the less of vital importance. The more I read scientific books on psychology the more I felt that the essential facts of experience were being missed out. In order to show how far it is possible to handle ideas with apparent competence and yet be utterly at sea in trying to live one's knowledge, I would like the reader to bear in mind, when reading the first few chapters, that I had a First Class Honours Degree in Psychology, and was also, during the time of this experiment, earning my living by applying my so-called psychological knowledge to others, in lecturing, research, and other ways. Actually it was the uneasy suspicion of this gap between knowing and living that determined the first steps in the developing of my method. Remembering Descartes, I set out to doubt everything I had been taught, but I did not try to rebuild my knowledge in a structure of logic and argument. I tried to learn, not from reason but from my senses. But as soon as I began to study my perception, to look at my own experience, I found that there were different ways of perceiving and that the different ways provided me with different facts. There was a narrow focus which meant seeing life as if from blinkers and with the centre of awareness in my head; and there was a wide focus which meant knowing with the whole of my body, a way of looking which quite altered my perception of whatever I saw. And I found that the narrow focus way was the way of reason. If one was in the habit of arguing about life it was very difficult not to approach sensation with the same concentrated attention and so shut out its width and depth and height. But it was the wide focus way that made me happy.

Having found this out my next task was to find what this wide focus depended upon, for I found I could not always achieve it. This led me to discover a part of my mind which I had never reckoned with before, to discover that whenever my thought was 'blind', that is, whenever I was not aware of what I was thinking, then my thoughts were liable to be quite childish and unreasonable. Of course in connexion with my professional work I had read many descriptions of the contents and habits of the 'unconscious mind' which by definition was something I could never by unaided effort know in myself. But I had not realized that the no-man's-land which lay between the dark kingdom of the psycho-analyst and the cultivated domain of my conscious thought was one which I could most profitably explore for myself. I had not realized that by a few simple tricks of observation I could become aware of quite unexpected things in myself. And it was gradually, by exploring this region, that I came to understand what forces were distorting and limiting my powers of perception, preventing me from making constant use of that source of happiness which my earlier observations had brought to light.

Although I continually came face to face with unexpected tendencies in myself, it was a long time before I found any theoretical terms in which to think about what might be happening. It was only after the attempt to review the course of my journey which is described in the main part of this book that I came upon a theory which shed light on some of my findings. Since my original aim was to present facts, not theories, I have tried to put forward this interpretation separately in the Epilogue. The following is a brief summary of the theory.

It seemed to me that my difficulties could most conveniently be considered in terms of a failure to understand that every human personality is two-sided, that every man or woman is potentially both male and female. It had not occurred to me that there were two fundamentally opposite and yet complementary tendencies in each of us, a polarity which determined the direction of every thought and feeling and extended far beyond what is ordinarily meant by a sexual relationship. So it seemed I had assumed that the only desirable way to live was a male way, I had tried to live a male life of objective understanding and achievement. Always, however, I had felt that this was not what really mattered to me, and as soon as I tried to question my experience I began to discover impulses towards a different attitude, impulses which eventually led me to find out something of the meaning of psychic femininity. Thus, part of my enterprise was concerned with the discovery that sex was far more than a physiological matter, though the more fully I understood this the more important also did the physical side become. It was no wonder that I had been able to find so little that was of use to me in scientific writings, for it now seemed, in the light of this theory of bisexuality, that the development of the feminine attitude beyond the purely physiological had never been intellectually understood. Since the developed feminine attitude naturally finds expression in terms of mysticism it had, I thought, been looked at askance by the analysing intellect and feared as an enemy of clear-headed detachment. Obviously, the hardest task for objective reasoning is to understand its opposite.

Most of the people I knew (both men and women) had made a cult of the 'male' intellect, that is, of objective reasoning as against subjective intuition. I had apparently been submissive towards this fashion and accepted its assumption that logical symbols were 'real', and anything else only 'wish-fulfilment'. So I had for years struggled to talk an intellectual language which for me was barren, struggled to force the feelings of my relation to the universe into terms that would not fit. For I had not understood at all that a feminine attitude to the universe was really just as legitimate, intellectually and biologically, as a masculine one; only, because it had never yet been properly understood, and had certainly not understood itself, it had always tended to give to its mythological and religious symbols a special reverence and validity. So I found that although the feminine or subjective attitude needs the male intellect if it is to understand itself, most of those I knew who possessed competent male intellects were not sufficiently both-sided themselves to have any notion of the meaning of subjectivity, whether in a man or a woman. Or some, who seemed to have partially understood their own femininity, like Weininger and D. H. Lawrence, hated and despised it because they were afraid of it. And I also had been afraid of it, had tried to fill my life with what were, for me, artificial male purposes. It seemed that my male side, unwilling to let go its purposes, had not dared give in to receptiveness, for it feared the loss of its own identity. And until it did I was unable to escape from that narrow focus of attention which always accompanied my purposiveness.

From all this I gathered that there are two entirely opposite attitudes possible in facing the problems of one's life. One, to try and change the external world, the other, to try and change oneself. Although both attitudes are potential in everyone, most of us have become one-sided, biased towards the preferred attitude in most of our dealings. To the man who is concerned with external matters, with trying to control people and things to suit his purposes, the problems of the opposite attitude seem morbid and unreal. While to him who has no desire to force his personality upon the world, who takes into himself what the external world has to offer and there remakes himself into a new being, the other attitude is apt to seem superficial – yet also something to be feared. But, at the same time as this mutual contempt and fear, there exists also in each of us a hankering after the opposite attitude, an unconscious attempt to restore the balance and become a

both-sided personality, complete like Plato's eight-limbed
beings who threatened to dethrone the gods.

So in my search I had found myself looking for ways of
learning how to think less about myself, just because I
found that such a one-sided approach was dull. This does
not mean, however, that it is everybody's good to think
less about themselves. Some, who are biased towards
perpetually giving themselves to external purposes, may
find their necessary balance in an opposite direction.

As for the method which led me to these discoveries,
let no one think it is an easy way because it is concerned
with moments of happiness rather than with stern duty
or high moral endeavour. For what is really easy, as I
found, is to blind one's eyes to what one really likes, to
drift into accepting one's wants ready-made from other
people, and to evade the continual day to day sifting of
values. And finally, let no one undertake such an experiment who is not prepared to find himself more of a fool
than he thought.

London, 1934

CHAPTER I

First Questions

A man that is born falls into a dream like a man who falls
into the sea. If he tries to climb out into the air as inex-
perienced people endeavour to do, he drowns — *nicht wahr?*
. . . No! I tell you! The way is to the destructive element
submit yourself, and with the exertions of your hands and
feet in the water make the deep, deep sea keep you up. . . .
In the destructive element immerse.

JOSEPH CONRAD

LOOKING back on the period when I began this undertaking I can distinguish two stages. In the first stage it
was gradually dawning on me that my life was not as I
would like it and that it might be in my power to make it
different. In the second stage I set about trying to find
what were the facts about it, as a preliminary to discovering how to make it different.

I cannot tell when the first stage began. All I can see
as I look back is a picture of myself going about my daily
affairs in a half-dream state, sometimes discontented but
never trying to find out why, vaguely 'making the best of
things', rarely looking ahead except casually, almost as a
game dreaming of what I would like to happen, but
never seriously thinking how I could set about to make
it happen. Usually I lived with a general feeling that all
would work out for the best, but this would be broken by
occasional outbursts of misery in which I felt quite
definitely that everything was hateful. These moments
never lasted very long. Usually after a night's rest I would
be back again in my vague optimism, never considering
that my life was my own to live, that if I did not manage it
as I wanted it no one else would. Into this smooth surface

of taking things for granted there began to emerge an awareness of certain mental discomforts which up till then I had not known, only suffered. What led me to become aware of them seems to have been a gradually growing habit of writing down my preoccupations. For when I began to consider my material for the present record I found random notes scattered amongst my papers, notes scribbled on the backs of envelopes, or on odd sheets. I was surprised at the vehemence of some of these effusions, for they seemed to reflect a state of mind which was very different from what I imagined about myself. I suppose now that, not being aware of my mental life, I was not aware of being miserable, for I never read through these notes, I simply wrote them in response to some blind impulse. But gradually they seem to have led me to realize that something was the matter.

Although I could not have told about it at the time, I can now remember the feeling of being cut off from other people, separate, shut away from whatever might be real in living. I was so dependent on other people's opinion of me that I lived in a constant dread of offending, and if it occurred to me that something I had done was not approved of I was full of uneasiness until I had put it right. I always seemed to be looking for something, always a little distracted because there was something more important to be attended to just ahead of the moment. At parties when I particularly wanted to make friends I often found myself unable to utter a word. Whatever I did I seemed never able to forget myself. There was an ever-present doubt, 'Am I doing this all right?'. I was not one of the people who could say, 'Of course I don't know anything about so-and-so, but I *do* know what I like.' I never did know.

This seemed to be an absurd state of affairs. But for a

long time I had no idea how to alter it. One day, however, prompted by a vague impulse, I began to try to write down what I wanted, not carefully considered aims, but just the first thing that came into my head. At first I seem to have produced only vague expressions of my sense of inadequacy.

I want to feel myself part of things, of the great drift and swirl: not cut off, missing things, like being sent to bed early as a child, the blinds being drawn while the sun and cheerful voices came through the chink from the garden.

I want companionship, another soul to hit back the ball of my thought: but often when I'm with people there's a fog and I can't. . . . How you long for people to say nice things about you.

Then, after attending a day's conference listening to discussions on how to improve the lot of the poor, I found I had written:

What I want is, not when I came to die to say, 'I've been as useful as I know how' – I ought to want that but I don't. I want to feel I have 'lived'. But what on earth do I mean by that? I mean something silly and Sunday paperish like 'plumbing the depths of human experience', or 'drinking life to the dregs'. What nonsense it sounds. I suppose I've got a Sunday paper mind. I don't want a life of service to a good cause, so it's no good pretending I do. Maybe it's colossal egotism, but I want a share in everything in the world, the bad as well as the good. The world is so marvellous, I want to grasp it, to partake of it, to embrace it, to feel every part of me vibrating with it. Do I? What are the things I want to share in?

This was astonishing. I could not understand why the language of these outpourings should be so different from my normal speech. In the circle in which I moved no extravagant expressions of emotion were tolerated, 'scenes' and heroics were alike taboo. Yet, here, as soon as I tried to find out what I wanted I could not get beyond these heroic phrases, and I could not answer this last question at all. But at least I seem to have been aware that these fine words did not get me much further, for there are signs in the next note that I was trying to be a little more specific.

Oh, I want to let go, to lose myself, my soul, what does it mean, to feel life pulsing through me, the big tides sweeping in, till I'm one with the immense surging fullness of the sea: and when it ebbs I would be clear and cool, washed free from stinking garbage and stagnant foetid water. What does all that mean? That when I read I'll forget my own personal self and feel the universe of the writer: that I'll let myself go at my purposes. Maybe I'll overshoot the mark, but does it matter? Whether it's getting a bit of work done or persuading someone to do what I want, or helping someone.

This was all very well, but it did not tell me *how* to let go, how to forget my personal self, what actually had to be done about it. I must have felt this lack and cast about for a remedy. For I remember that I often had an impulse to go into the slums and forget myself in trying to lessen the troubles of others; but always I was held back by doubts, doubts whether I really had anything to give, doubts whether it was any use trying to help others towards a way of life which I myself was finding so unsatisfactory. Then I thought that perhaps I would find that essence of life which was eluding me if I was myself forced up against the hard facts of poverty, so I often dreamed of setting out to live in the underworld. But here caution and cowardice prevailed and also my common sense was sceptical of anything which approached the romantically dramatic. Then psycho-analysis was inevitably suggested. But at that time I did not see how it could be arranged, and also it seemed to me too privileged a way out; I thought I wanted to find something that was available for everyone. Finally, I seem to have considered what was, amongst some of my acquaintances, the fashionable cure for all such troubles as mine, for I find the following note:

Why not? Why won't you live with him? Fear of the letting go and giving up. Breaking down the walls of one's fantasy and privacy: of being outcast from the family, of being found out in sin. . . .

But I hate to be blocked, closed, shut, I want all the life of the universe flowing through me. I suppose I would if it was a desert island. Now it seems like a giving up of all one's world, a plunge. Is the fact that I don't love him an excuse for fear? Or an intuitive safeguarding wisdom?

This indecision marks the end of the first phase. I had opened my eyes to the fact that my life was not as I would like. But what was I to do about it? Would taking a lover be a cure-all? Was I to trust the general assumption amongst a certain set of my own generation that it would, or was I to believe in the standards I had been brought up with and be shocked at the very idea? This was only a particular example of the whole problem. If my life was not satisfactory as it was, in what way was I to change it? By what standard was I to guide it?

Here I began to consider by what standards I had been guiding it. If I could find that out then I might know what to avoid in the future. Here, though I did not guess it at the time, was a most important step, for instead of trying to force myself into doing what I imagined I ought to do I began to enquire into what I was doing. I little knew what this apparently simple act of trying to be aware of my own experience would involve me in.

My first attempt was a consideration of all the things that I seemed to be aiming at . . . being good at one's job, pleasing people, being popular, not missing things, doing what's expected of one, not letting people down, helping people, being happy. As soon as I began to think about it

I saw that whichever of these aims might be the most important to work for I would not achieve it; for my life was determined, not by any one of them, but by a planless mixture of them all. I discovered that I was drifting without rudder or compass, swept in all directions by influence from custom, tradition, fashion, swayed by standards uncritically accepted from my friends, my family, my countrymen, my ancestors. Were these reliable guides for one's life? I could not assume that they were, for everywhere around me I saw old ways of doing things breaking down and proving inadequate. Not only was it that I felt dubious about trusting the dictates of a social tradition which had landed us in the war, but the voice of that tradition was so confused that I did not in fact know what it was telling me to do, what sort of life it did require of me. But what else was there? If I was neither to do simply what other people did, nor just what was expected of me, what guide was there? My own reason? But I had long since found that I did not know enough, I had not the mental capacity to follow a logical argument far enough to reach any conclusions which I felt certain about. It always seemed too easy to prove what one wanted to prove for me to feel any confidence in reason alone. Also, if I was to argue out for myself the best way to live and base my whole life on my conclusions must I not begin with a clear understanding of the nature of the universe? Must I therefore read all the latest pronouncements of science before I could get on with my own life? Even if I did and could understand them, how would I know which one to choose as a basis of life, when so many disagreed? Here I was filled with misgivings lest I must wait to find happiness till I could live reasonably and to live reasonably till I could understand Einstein and make a critical analysis of biological theory. But was it any good trying, for experts in reason had told me that in any case the conclusions of the plain man upon the ultimate nature of the universe were not worthy of serious consideration? But if not reason, wha' else? Was there no intuitive sense of how one should live, something like the instinct which prompts a dog to eat grass when he feels ill? Though I knew such an idea was looked upon with suspicion I felt it was a possibility not to be ignored. Perhaps such a sense would make itself felt through one's spontaneous wants. Or perhaps such a sense, though it did exist, had become dulled by our present ways of living so that some wants were idle, mere imitation, but underneath were a different kind having a real relation to one's fundamental needs. Or perhaps this last kind of want, this sense of what was important for oneself, could be developed by practice, just as one's sense of what is a good or bad picture can be.

Then it struck me that perhaps being happy might really be the indication for such a sense. Perhaps if one really knew when one was happy one would know the things that were necessary for one's life? On the other hand perhaps happiness was quite irrelevant, perhaps one had to go for what one wanted not minding how unpleasant it was.

Since I was suspicious of my own power of reasoning I decided it was no good trying to answer these questions by sitting down and thinking them out. Neither would I read what other people had said, for although I knew there were plenty who wanted to tell me how I should direct my life I could not be sure that what might be right for them would also be right for me. Instead, I decided to look at the facts of my own life, to see if I could find out what I wanted to know simply by observation and experiment. I thought that I would try to observe

what my wants were and whether I got them and
whether it made me happy or not. I thought the best
way to begin was to keep a diary, noting in it every day
when I had been particularly happy and anything that
I wanted. At the same time I would note anything else
that seemed important so that if it should turn out that
happiness did not matter I should have a chance of finding out what was more important.

Although I was quite certain that I must find some
way of observing the facts of my life, it took me a long
time to make this plan and to decide just what to put in
my diary. I had tried to keep diaries before, but only for
a few weeks, always getting a little bored with writing
down everything that happened. I did in fact make the
experiment again this time, just choosing one ordinary
working day and trying to record what had been in my
mind. The result horrified me. I was quite dismayed to
discover the depths of my own self-absorption, and
thought that if my daily record meant writing down this
sort of thing I could never keep it up. Here is what I
wrote:

My main concern when I got up this morning was whether
I'd be able to get my hair cut before going to work: and
whether I wasn't looking pale and tired, and how limp I felt,
almost unable to cope with going to see F. I was in the depths
when I rang up the hairdresser and he couldn't see me. . . . I
was cheered by finding the S. street place would cut my hair:
and having it done by a polite young man. At the office I hoped
there'd be someone about to see how nicely my hair was cut,
and how attractive it looked. On combing it I thought how
plain I was. Then I lunched with F. and had no leisure for
thinking of my looks, except when I knew I was flushed and had
he noticed it. I left him in a glow of elation that all had gone so
well, thinking what an intriguing person I was. After a bit of
work, not very concentrated, and an attempt to find Miss P.
and show her my new hair-cut, I chatted to her and thought

how charming I had been. I went to the club and was delighted to hear M. say my hair looked charming. We played ping-pong and playing better than usual I thought I was a fine creature. . . . At supper . . . I wondered whether I was talking well, and when they mentioned M. I felt a slap in the face because he'd sent a p.c. to someone else: also sort of hurt because they said he wasn't strong and mightn't stand roughing it. I hated to think these people knew him. They might guess that I'd taken him seriously, and knew that I was only one of many for him. But I think none of them really understood him and I did. I came home and sorted photos to put in a book, picking out those that were good of me. Good God!

This observation nearly made me abandon my enterprise altogether. Exhortations were continually in the back of my mind as a criticism and a reproach: 'Think less about yourself', 'Don't be so self-absorbed', 'Think about other people and you'll have no time for your own worries'. I became filled with doubts. Wasn't this attempt to examine the facts of my own life likely to land me further into the bog of introspection? This was the last thing I wanted, for I found a note scribbled at this time:

The other day I thought the only thing that mattered was seeing the other person's point of view – the man of widest sympathies.

And three weeks later there is an unfinished sentence:

If I haven't the wits to discover something, once and always, that I love more and that matters more, than myself . . .

According to the code I had absorbed from childhood, o be dubbed selfish was the worst thing I knew. I had, accepted the somewhat negative idea of unselfishness as the ultimate goal of all my childish efforts to be good. I do not think I ever critically considered just what I meant by unselfishness, but now the word awakens a picture of continual restlessness in which someone is always half rising from the most comfortable chair in the room and saying, '*Do* sit here.' In later years I was always trying to force myself to think more about other people, always making resolutions and expecting the desired behaviour to follow from my act of will. But I had only grown more and more shut within myself. For years I had blundered on, always assuming that it was my weakness of will that was at fault, for it never occurred to me that I might be using the wrong method. Now at last, however, I began to guess that I could not vanquish my egoism by running away from it. I must 'in the destructive element immerse'.

Thus it was that I began a task which has absorbed my efforts for many years: trying to manage my life, not according to tradition, or authority, or rational theory, but by experiment.

At the beginning of my diary I copied out the following passage:

> Our ignorance of the goal and purport of human life, and the mistrust we are apt to feel of the guidance of the spiritual sense, on account of its proved readiness to accept illusions as realities, warn us against deductive theories of conduct.*

I was not at all clear what this implied especially as I never could remember what 'deductive' meant, yet I felt that some warning was needed. It was not until years later, when I read it again, that it occurred to me that the writer might be talking of private and public reality as though they were the same thing. So I thought that I had perhaps been right in my feeling that the quotation contained a warning for me, but I did not think it was the one the writer intended. If he meant by spiritual sense something that was not based on rational argument, something that one knew but did not know how one

*Francis Galton in *Inquiries into Human Faculty*.

knew, then surely one must distinguish the sphere in which this sense was to apply. I felt it was wise to be afraid of being gulled by ideas about the external world that were not based on reason but were only products of my own desires, but I must not let this fear run away with me and blind me to the possibility of there being a direct sense of what was real in my internal universe, a sense which reasoned analysis might only blur. Public reality, what was agreed fact about the external world, did not seem able to tell me what was important for me, or what to do in order to live in accordance with the laws of my own being. But might there not perhaps be a private reality, a reality of feeling rather than of knowing, which I could not afford to ignore? As far as I knew science had not considered this other domain, had sometimes said it did not exist, sometimes merely said it was there but was not any concern of the scientist. But although science repudiated it, could I not borrow some useful hints from her in learning how to manage it? I knew well that these questions of desire and happiness were too fleeting, too personal to be caught in the precise formulae which science demanded, but could I not at least apply the methods of experiment, learn to observe, make my own hypotheses and check them up against further observations of my private reality?

I must have known vaguely what lay ahead of me, for I still have a crumpled piece of paper with a quotation which I had copied out, and which I now remember carrying about in my pocket at this time:

This soul, or life within us, by no means agrees with the life outside us. If one has the courage to ask her what she thinks, she is always saying the very opposite to what other people say. . . . Really she is the strangest creature in the world, far from heroic, variable as a weathercock, 'bashful, insolent; chaste, lustful; prating, silent; laborious, delicate; ingenious, heavy; melancholic, pleasant; lying, true; knowing, ignorant; liberal, covetous, and prodigal' – in short, so complex, so indefinite, corresponding so little to the version which does duty for her in public, that a man might spend his life in merely trying to run her to earth.*

*

My determination to write an account of this search had begun from the conviction that unless I wrote about it I would lose my way. Yet for years I hesitated, not knowing in what form to tell it. I shrank from the thought of a direct personal account of what happened to me, yet knew all the time that only as such could it have any value to others. I was tempted to write my experience as the story of what happened to a friend, an imaginary character, for the tradition of reticence in which I was born and bred was hard to fight against. What helped me most was the gradually growing conviction that silence might be the privilege of the strong but it was certainly a danger to the weak. For the things I was prompted to keep silent about were nearly always the things I was ashamed of, which would have been far better aired and exposed to the cleansing winds of confession. I knew then that though my decision to write in direct personal terms would lead me on to dangerous ground yet it was the very core of my enterprise. For I had often thought that novelists and poets had a special advantage in learning how to live, their writings providing them with an instrument that most of us were denied. By being able to dramatize their own difficulties they were in a far better position for solving them. But if one had no gift for creating imaginative truth, for symbolizing the stresses and strains of one's own inner life in terms of sound and shape or invented happenings to others, was

*Virginia Woolf, essay on Montaigne in *The Common Reader*.

there no way of dealing with them? Of course there were
books on psychology, handbooks telling one how to be
happy, successful, well-balanced, thousands of words of
exhortation about how one ought to live. But these were
all outside me; they seemed too remote, they spoke in
general terms and it was so hard to see how they applied
in special cases; it was so fatally easy to evade their demands on oneself. Was there not a way by which each
person could find out for himself what he was like, not by
reading what other people thought he ought to be, but
directly, as directly as knowing the sky is blue and
how an apple tastes, not needing anyone to tell him?
Perhaps, then, if one could not write for other people
one could write for oneself, and perhaps draw for
oneself.

One point I feel might serve particularly as a warning
to any who may be tempted to set out, armed with a
pencil and a sixpenny note-book, on a similar enterprise.
It concerns the reading of books. For a long time I was
continually putting off the next step in my exploration
because I felt I ought to know more, knew there were
many books written about these things, felt that I must
read them all before I could go any further. Whenever I
gave in to this impulse I found it disastrous. It took me
years to learn that I must never begin my search by looking in books, never say, 'I know too little, I must read
some more before I start', but that I must always observe
first, express what I observed, and then, if I needed it,
see what the books had to say. Because of this discovery
there will not be many references to books in the following chapters. I wish to emphasize this point particularly
because, although before making this decision I had
tried to read a good deal of current literature about the
mind, it had always completely damped my enthusiasm

for discovery, leaving me in despair with a burden of guilt because there was so much I did not understand. Finally I decided only to read books that would keep my heart up, books that would give me the mood I wanted rather than information. Yet because I was daunted by the imposing array of printed information I must not minimize my debt to it. Probably reading has influenced my thought far more than I know, although at the time I may have seen no connexion between what I read and the intimate problems which were haunting me. But if learned books, with some important exceptions, only seemed to delay me, conversation provided certain ideas and a view-point without which I should most certainly have lost my way in a maze of uncertainties. Here I cannot tell at all where my debt ends. Since the best teacher shows the way to finding things out for oneself it is impossible to say how much of the work is the pupil's own. So it happened that many of those apparent discoveries which burst upon me with a shock of delight turned out to be applications of ideas which I had been told already but had not fully understood.

There is another point. I have often wondered whether what I have called my discoveries may be true only for me. My path may have wandered through deserts and waste places which may be quite off the main highway. The records of how one traveller who has missed his way struggled back on to the right road are not interesting to those who knew which way to go from the beginning. To these, stories of strange birds seen in remote marshes may seem to be only the products of a distorted imagination. That I cannot tell, for in going through these records I have sometimes thought that my difficulties must seem childish to most people I know, but then again remembered how easy it is to slip into the mistake of imagining oneself to be unique. Certainly, however, in the later stages of what I had thought was a lonely trail I came upon the outskirts of a country which seemed to be well known to the few, though little spoken of and I think unguessed at by the many.

CHAPTER II

Keeping a Diary

My next work was to view the country, and seek a proper place for my habitation, and where to stow my goods to secure them from whatever might happen. Where I was I yet knew not, whether on the continent or on an island; whether inhabited or not inhabited; whether in danger of wild beasts or not. There was a hill not above a mile from me, which rose up very steep and high, and which seemed to overtop some other hills, which lay as in a ridge from it northward. I took out one of the fowling pieces, and one of the pistols, and a horn of powder, and thus armed, I travelled for discovery up to the top of that hill, where, after I had with great labour and difficulty got up, I immediately saw my fate, to my great affliction; viz. that I was in an island, environed every way with the sea, no land to be seen, except some rocks, which lay a great way off, and two small islands less than this, which lay about three leagues to the west.

DANIEL DEFOE

WHEN I set out to keep a diary of what I wanted and of what made me happy I had the idea that it would be a kind of preliminary mental account-keeping. It was in December, 1926, and I expected that after a few weeks or months I would be able to say: 'These are the facts of my life, now I'm going to take it in hand for myself and do something about it.'

I began on a Sunday. This was the only day when I had leisure enough to catch up with the smaller necessities of my life, darning, writing letters, general tidying-up. By the end of the day all I could find to say in my diary was: 'Rather oppressed with the number of things to be done.' The only special happiness that I could remember was hearing someone playing the piano in the distance and watching the splashing water in my bath.

The next day, back at my work, I apparently had only one moment which seemed important. It was a moment of absent-mindedness when I looked up from my desk and found myself gazing at grey roofs and chimneys, a view typical from a million of London's top-floor windows. I do not remember exactly what I saw but only the shock of delight in just looking.

On the following day I recorded good moments in listening to music on the wireless, bits of *Hänsel und Gretel*, someone explaining about music and playing simple chords, Handel's 'Lament of Samson on his blindness'. The next day, recorded the morning after, has only this brief entry: 'Mostly pleasure in people liking you.'

Then there were two unrecorded days, dismissed on the evening of the third with: 'Bad days, no impulse to write, cold in the head, constipated, too much to eat. Too tired to think of any wants. Restless. I don't know what I want except to emerge from this lotus land of dreaming.'

Here was a week gone and there did not seem to be very much which was important in my life, or if there were important things I was not seeing them.

Perhaps these days have been unsatisfactory, unreal, because I've been avid for happiness, drifting into those things either that have before given happiness, or that require little effort. Perhaps that's why holidays are sometimes unhappy: you hunt happiness directly, so lose it. Or perhaps it's only that you've been constipated and eaten too much. Your sense of what will bring happiness is so crude and blundering. Try something else as a compass. Maybe the moralists are right and happiness doesn't come from seeking pleasure and ease. What then shall I seek to-morrow?

Apparently I 'could not think of an answer to this question and I seem to have been so discouraged by the first week's results that I wrote nothing for eight days, except that under the heading of 'wants' I had recorded that I wished I could meet a young man I knew. I remember that I went to a tea-shop where I had met him once, hoping he might come again, but I did not record this in the diary.

In spite of my disappointment with such meagre findings I seem to have been convinced that I was setting about my task in the right way, for on January 4th I began again:

Sudden bursts of laughter together make me happy, at . . but this evening, reading aloud to N., who is in bed, I was happy at hearing her laugh. . . . I remembered a rush of enthusiasm at the thought of being a loyal friend – most uplifting – though I can't remember when. I'm very easily uplifted.

On the following day I attended a lecture about modern methods in a girls' prison. I wrote:

Pleasure in feeling a useful and important person after listening to Miss B.'s lecture. Has she the gift of making everyone feel like that?

I do not seem to have enlarged upon the thought of how odd it was that I should feel a glow of usefulness in merely listening to accounts of other people's hard work.

On January 6th I made a list of 'wants':

– a sign of affection from H. I did not get it, at least not for certain, and now I'm not quite sure that I want it, he knows too much.
– a pair of red shoes. I tried some on but they were too small. I still want some.
– listening to a lecture I wanted to get on with this diary tonight. This evening I didn't feel like it and read . . . now I want to know what P. and D. said about me; but I don't mind very much.

On the 11th I wrote:

I've discovered where a great part of my thought goes. I was thinking about my new frock and red shoes.

On the 14th I began to have doubts about what I was
doing:

I don't think this diary is much good if it only records feelings. It should be a motive for experiment as well as observation. I want – now, while wondering what I want, the patterns
and colourings on the vase on my table took on a new and intense vitality – I want to be so harmonious in myself that I can
think of others and share their experiences.

On the 15th I wrote:

Last night I was sick of mental things and self-observation.
I saw the exhibition of Flemish pictures but felt they spoke a
strange language and only occasionally could I catch the gist
of what they said – a Van der Weyden Madonna and Child, in
tones of mellow autumn sunlight, two Rubens figures in a small
sketch, irradiating immense vigour and energy, scraps of striking harmonies of colour – I wanted someone to interpret them.

In reading through my diary I can now see what I
did not notice at the time, that the effort of recording
my experiences was having an influence upon their
nature. I was beginning to take notice of and seek ways
of expressing occurrences which had before been lost in
vagueness. I find the following record for the 16th:

I heard J. T. play at her house: César Franck, 'Prelude, Aria
and Fugue', Mozart Sonata in C (?), Chopin, Scriabine, and
while I tried to listen clamouring demons surrounded me,
deafening me, shouting: 'This is not for you, you are a
shrunken and imprisoned creature, your emotions are only
poor pale imitations, never can this glorious flood of great feeling sweep through you and absorb you.' I fought them and
then had a picture of a queer creature lying dead, quite colourless, looking most like a 'foetal dragon'. For an instant I joined
in the highest triumph of the music and I saw the creature who
wouldn't let me listen before as a poor, shrunken thing, easy
to throw off. By attending to him – or 'it', rather, it is not
worthy of a more personal pronoun – it becomes a bloated
brute, weighing down your life.

I wrote this down, feeling it was an odd experience, but had no notion what it was all about and never thought of it again. The diary goes on as before:

17th. What ever you do, do it like Hell. Oh, I did love the Astaires in *Lady be Good*. I wanted to make something more of my work but didn't know how to begin. I wanted that £3:10s. hat terribly.

18th. It was a little difficult to do it like Hell when the doing was tramping the streets with Mr B. or listening while he coped with hurried interviews or to do it when having supper with H. Do what? Make him love me? But I'm not sure that I want him to. I want, not power, like H., or domination, but to share things, experiences, not passively, as if sitting at a theatre all one's life, but actively taking part in things.

19th. Too darned cold to write. Going to bed.

20th. I found the bit of stuff I wanted for a coat but there wasn't enough of it and I felt bitterly thwarted.

22nd. At the Zoo. Joy of long red legs and yellow ones, in a sudden run, like a trill, a dance, some quaint little plover – and the other day a pigeon glided down over my shoulder, the movement like sudden music. Joy in the animals and joy in the desirelessness of shapes. Afternoon, boredom, indigestion, and ecstasy over a Holst, 'St Paul's Suite'. This is of me. I know it, a language I can understand without striving – and a Bach concert like the Day of Judgement.

23rd. Exulted in my body and clothes and red skirt and freedom to do as I chose on Sunday morning. After lunch headache and sleep. Evening delight in Chapter I of *Ulysses*. Some queer spell that gives the sense of humanity – like the trance from reading 'The Hound of Heaven' when I was twelve. Pleasure in my room, 'Ain't I a fine fellow!' I want – to be carried in the stream because the stream is bigger than I am.

26th. I made a new game. Watching people in buses and tubes and guessing where they bought their clothes. This led me to a building up of their personalities, their interests, their purposes at the moment. I found here escape from self, poise. . . . It's weak and despicable to go on wanting things and not trying to get them. Talk to M. It won't matter if he does think you a forward ass. I want – a lover.

Then I began to reconsider what I was trying to do.

28th. This diary is to discover where one can put one's faith, as shown by experience. Also where one does put one's faith. One can't put it in the physical forces of nature – drowning or falling or burning – one's death may be sheer accident. Some people believe there's no such thing and that God wills a ship to sink or a thunderstorm.

Can one put it in the voice of the herd, tradition, accepted codes?

Can one put it in any body of doctrine expounded by men? e.g. Church teaching?

Can one put it in one's own reasoning power or logic?

Can one put it in desire, all passionate desire?

Can one put it in satisfaction, 'sense of reality'?

Then what is to be the criterion of the success of your faith? Happiness, satisfaction, feeling of worthwhileness?

But I think happiness is like effect on an audience (when acting), if you think of it all the time you will not get it, you must get lost in the part, lost in your purposes and let the effect be the criterion of your success.

Can you guide your wants by each of these in turn and see which brings happiness?

Snags: there are too many variables and probably you must live by them all in various degrees.

I think particular is safer than general, guessing where a particular woman bought her hat and writing down a particular day-dream is more useful than the above attempted logical analysis.

I did not think that this had got me much further but the problem remained in my thoughts.

29th. In the night was a gale and I lay awake, clear-headed. I began to think of all my doings throughout the day and whether any of them were a direct outcome of a belief in God. I found none. But I'd only got half through the day when I went to sleep. In connexion with yesterday's ideas it came into my head, 'But the Lord was not in the fire',

'But the Lord was not in the wind',

'And after the wind a still small voice'.

But I did not know about any 'still small voice' so I continued with my search.

I think pains and hatreds should go in this diary too. I could
hardly bear the parts of the Heath where I walked with B.
though I had loved them before.

A brooding fear of Industry, its drabness, petty competition,
and huge forceful machines – Caliban.

Feb. 2nd. Absorbed in my own gloom until the lunch hour
when Lincoln's Inn in the misty sun made me think 'What does
it matter how I feel!'

Then I remembered feeling jealous of J. when M. talked to
her, and all my other jealousies and how I won't own up to
myself about unpleasant feelings so I think I'm colourless,
emotionless. Coming home late I thought how my list of
'wants' was a very censored one, only those that my 'self' ap-
proves of. I must make another – giving very specific 'wants',
e.g. at the Club I wanted T. to be thinking 'What a charming
and interesting-looking girl' although I hate his voice and face.

I want to see something clearly and hang on to it.

I seem to have continued brooding over 'the still small
voice', for on February 4th there is a note of something –
'that tells me in spite of the clatter of the crowd, "This is
ludicrous, absurd", "That is stupendous, immense".'
On the 5th there's a note, 'What's the good of all this!'
and on the 9th, 'I liked the smooth roundness of my body
in my bath but would like someone else to like it'; and on
February 11th:

Like a fierce wind roaring high up in the bare branches of
trees, a wave of passion came over me, aimless but surging. . . .
I suppose it's lust but it's awful and holy like thunder and
lightning and the wind. All day I've been haunted by the
thought that we are like the bobbing corks fishermen tie to
their nets at sea – each a little insignificant bit. – So you've
thought – what have you done, a little work, a little vague chat?

Feb. 14th. In the night I felt cold all over and everything I
thought was fearful and sinister with a queer veil of horror between me and all I looked on – like the twilight of the sun's
eclipse. I just waited to let it pass, keeping a close grip on myself, but immovable. There were queer ghoulish phantoms doing
acrobatic tricks and I could remember no pleasant things. Then

I remembered the house near R. where I stayed as a child and was homesick and miserable.

On the 16th there begin to be more observations of surroundings. I was doing temporary work in a Midland factory.

The foreman, in order to make the Frenchman understand English, shouts loudly in his ear as if he were deaf.

The full moon *does* sail as you walk.

This (recording the important moments of the day) makes me think of counting over the day's spoils, little pink shells and treasures from the shore.

Feb. 18th. Rush of work . . . it seems so unreal, all the time I wonder, 'Is it worth it?' I suppose the vital things are not really excluded from factory work but they seem so. But the girls sing at their work and the boys play the fool in the D. Room – perhaps it's only the bosses that have lost or hidden their souls in a cupboard.

Feb. 19th. Community singing at the Cup Tie, like a single voice, the voice of a . . . beast-god. Its moods, first sleepy and sentimental when singing, then roused to fierceness in a shout of 'FOUL!' There was an accident and as the man lay still on the ground my neighbour said, 'It was his HEAD!' in an awed voice, repeating it again and again. And I shared with him the horrid thrill at the thought of a broken neck.

40,000 men singing 'God save the King' with immense fervour.

Directed towards what? The little Guelf man?

All ye like sheep have gone astray.

I don't know what I want. I'm a cork bobbing on the tide.

On the 22nd there is a note:

What to put? What am I after?
'I wish I were a cassowary
On the plains,' etc. etc. . . .

I thought it over and over in the train from Birmingham and found it most soothing.

Here was the first hint about the possible effects of controlling one's thoughts, but I did not realize its importance at the time. For I was busy with other problems.

Feb. 23rd. One day I'll make a list of points of conflict with the herd. One is – 'They' assume that what happens is what matters, where you go, what you do, things that happen, the good time that you have. But often I believe it's none of these things, it's the times between, the long days when nothing happens, the odd moments, perhaps when you open a letter, or sit alone in a restaurant, or exchange the time of day with a stranger. . . .

Actually this was not the first time I had had an idea of this sort for on January 6th I had put:

Possibly the thing that matters, that you are looking for, is like the roots of plants, hidden and happening in the gaps of your knowledge.

But if it was not to be known, what good was it to me? At that time I had no technique for taking into account what might be in the gaps of my knowledge.

The note for February 23rd continues:

I walked on a dark country road with glimmers of sunset under a hail-storm sky, and wind and Orion clear in a light patch of sky, and laughed till the tears came just at being alive.

It was now six weeks since I began and certain changes of aim were emerging.

I have said that when I first began to keep this diary I had intended to look at my life as a preliminary to deciding what I should do to make it as I wanted. But when I actually began to keep a record of daily concerns I was disappointed to find that this preliminary step was not as easy as I had expected. For I then came to realize that the facts of my life were not so many fixed items which only needed adding up and balancing. They were rather the continually receding horizons of the traveller who climbs a mountain. Writing down my experiences then seemed to be a creative act which continually lit up new possibilities in what I had seen. Of course I could not at that time have put this discovery into words: I merely felt that it was useless to go over these records as I had originally planned in order to balance up the happiness and make decisions how to act in future. Instead I felt an urge to go on and on writing, with my interest gradually shifting from what to do with my life to how to look at it. There is a note for instance on February 28th which shows that one of the problems which had bothered me was apparently solving itself without any deliberate action on my part.

Some serenity and a sense of not being – 'outside life' – but of – 'being life' – one's hopes and fears and strivings.

I was also discovering other aspects of the problem of action and effort, for on the same day I wrote:

I lost myself in a Schubert Quartet at the end of a Crowndale Road concert, partly by ceasing all striving to understand the music, partly by driving off intruding thoughts, partly feeling the music coming up inside me, myself a hollow vessel filled with sound.

There seem to be more happy moments too, although my first recognition of the spring was a bit grudging:

March 2nd. There's a crocus up and the buds are swelling but the spring makes a waste inside me – not dead but alive enough to feel its empty ache. Is it all because there's no news of B.?
March 4th. Happy at work, fairly, Club Dance, H. happy in rhythm and movement, home at 4 a.m.
March 8th. A gleaming March day, happy doing routine work at the office, happy to be in the stream of things, 'in the destructive element immerse', to feel it go over my head, hopes and fears, joys and sorrows.

I now began to observe other things:

March 9th. I want self-forgetfulness, but I believe I've been wanting to remember to admire while I forget – wanting to have my cake and eat it.

March 10th. I realized how completely untrustworthy I am in personal relationships, how I take one attitude when with one person and an opposite one with the next person, always agreeing with the person present.

March 18th. At the Zoo . . . a red-legged peewit, his crest erect, tense and tumultuous, and a little boy in a sailor suit dancing and skipping by himself on his way to look at the sea-lions.

I thought what an awful thing is idealism when reality is so marvellous.

March 19th. This morning I felt I wanted no lover, of myself I could face reality without a high priest to intervene

March 26th. The other day I was envious of the B.'s beginning holidays and I noticed that when I envy other people I think their good fortune is sheer luck, but when other people envy me I think – 'Yes – but – well, of course, I deserve it!'

As I came out of Y. School in the dark drizzle there were two little urchins squeezed behind the iron gate, talking in loud whispers. The fun of getting in a corner of one's own choosing, hidden, even if damp and uncomfortable.

March 27th. In bed I tried to find the spiritual life that D. R. knows. I read a booklet on 'Self-preparation' but was filled with doubt.

I went on the Heath and watched the ragged urchins trawling for minnows with an old sack. That's what I love – the grass, sodden with winter rains, the squelch of mud under foot, the ripples round the paddling urchins, the splash of water, a mist of green buds. Oh God, I love these things fiercely, they are familiar and intimate. And I am afraid of the spiritual life and the spiritual teachings – I want to understand and grasp these little things, and individual people.

March 31st. Too tired to write all this week. On Monday I met a man I liked at a dance, J., and was a little scared at getting to know him quickly. I was happy all next day because he liked me and we had made friends quickly. I looked up his name in the telephone book and there were hundreds of J.'s! ! I remembered doing that for B. and for S. ! ! . . . At the Club I was cross because I talked to no one. R. sat beside me on the sofa and giggled at *Punch*. From embarrassment I asked for a match, went to get my cigarettes and when I came back found someone had taken my place. I was half relieved, half annoyed and

jealous of B., who could talk (and win a doubtful reputation?).
What price the spiritual life? These are the things that fill one's
day. . . .

I'm writing this so when I'm 60 I'll not forget how I felt.

Wants

April 1st.

To think out why I can't 'get at people'.

To hear from S. about America – he came and told me.

To buy silk for underclothes – I bought it. And plaited
shoes – I ordered them.

For O. to come and talk to me – he didn't.

To buy silk stockings – I bought the wrong ones.

To make S. think I'm not so innocent as I look – in fact,
rather a woman of the world – did I?

To get in touch with J. – I got his initials from the College.

To make love with someone I loved – I didn't because there
wasn't anyone.

To find a letter from B. – there wasn't.

April 8th. H. talks wisely to me about complicated physics, I
say 'Oh yes' and am duly impressed, but he may be quite wrong
for all I know – he can bluff and swank as much as he likes.
Then I do the same to someone else, and tell a lot of knowing
rot – so it goes on.

About this time I came upon many new experiences.
Up to now I had been determined to examine my experience in order to find out where and why it was inadequate. Now, when new things were beginning to
happen to me, I seem to have felt, for a time at least, that
the experience was enough in itself and that it was better
simply to live it, since looking at it too deliberately might
spoil it. So, although the diary continues, somewhat in-
termittently, it becomes more a simple record of external
happenings than a deliberate attempt to evaluate and
understand them.

Some of my new experiences were physical ones, and I
think I was particularly reluctant to record these for two
reasons. First, I found words so inadequate to convey the

quality of what happened and that they even sometimes had the power to destroy what they could not express. Second, these moments of physical happiness were emerging from a new direction. Up to now the incidents which I had felt impelled to select for each day's record had been moments of clearer consciousness, whereas now my experience was a plunge into a darker region. Yet although I could not bring myself to observe this new awareness, I did feel there was a tremendous amount to be learnt in it, and in some way I seem to have understood that by persisting in my study of the moments of clear-headed happiness I would eventually reach a more real understanding of the passionate ones.

June 7th. We have been camping by the Thames at Goring. . . . I smelt the young corn in the evening and the dusty road and nettles in the hedge. In the mornings I lay beside D. and sometimes slept or watched the swifts circling high up against a pale sky, their wings gold-bronze when catching the early sun. D.'s touch soothed me, giving peace through my body. . . . All this time since Easter I have felt life flowing all around me and over my head – and I am happy being immersed.

June 8th. I want us to travel together, exploring, seeing how people live, talking to queer people by the roadside, sleeping at country inns, sailing boats, tramping dusty roads. . . .

. . . to learn to understand the intricacies of his personality, like a piece of music – fitting the bits together – the connecting themes and central purpose.

Then to have him as a support and buttress to rely on for judgement and understanding, and someone to contend with. . . .

To give up to the creative chemistry and live amongst things that grow – a child, a garden and quietness.

Fears and Drawings-back

Of being tied up, of limiting my will, no longer a 'mobile unit' to come and go as I choose.

Of limitations in future friendships. . . .

*

I used to trouble about what life was for – now being alive seems sufficient reason.

June 18th. I want –

Time, leisure to draw and study a few things closely by feeling, not thinking – to get at things.

I want laughter, its satisfaction and balance and wide security.

I want a chance to play, to do things I choose just for the joy of doing, for no purpose of advancement.

To understand patiently the laws of growing things. I feel there is no time for these because I am driven by the crowd, filling my days with earning money, and keeping up with friends – like a ping-pong ball.

July 20th. I plan my wedding frock often. I think of it as the most marvellous garment that ever was! A vague 'better than anything I've seen'.

September 17th. To-day several of us walked through Golders Hill Gardens. There was a swan on the pond. Then I felt a sudden immense reality with D. The swans and reeds had a 'thusness', 'so and no otherwise' existing in an entirely different sphere from the world of opinion.

September 20th. Yesterday I saw quite clearly (but now my head swims when I try to think of it) that the realness I feel with D. is because we supply mutual needs. Apart from my need for a man and his for a woman, we can understand each other, and he can give a certain vigour, headstrongness. . . .

I feel by having him I can plunge more into life and take part in the business of living, home-making, earning, discovery. Even a suburban existence would be exciting, experimenting to see what we could make of the universal problems.

Travelling would be fun but it would be mostly studying other people's struggles, standing aloof – while I want to plunge into the thick of it, not to be always tourists in life.

And think I have got things to give him. I can help him to adapt, to co-ordinate his energies, to achieve more poise without losing vigour. Sometimes I have been angry with his arrogances – just as I have been angry when people are ill – and think I have only to tell him and he will change as I please. But I think I can learn to understand what he is getting at – often blindly, in spite of his insight. I feel now sometimes that I am inextricably bound up with his growth. I feel we have picked each other from the crowd as fellow-travellers, for neither of us is to the other's personality the end-all and the be-all. We are both after something (God knows what) and feel instinctively we can help each other towards it. I would like the relationship to give the greatest possible freedom to both of our personalities.

I dream now of riding, sun-bathing, skiing in California, of meeting many kinds of people and making friends, of tracking down new ideas on human problems, of living in the country with a mulberry tree in the garden . . . of wandering abroad with rucksacks, sitting at little tables under trees.

I feel we are young together, immensely young.

September 21st, 12 p.m. My last night alone in bed for many a day. It seems 'putting off of childish things' to have someone to love. Yet I was hoping together we might be more childlike, less oppressed with cares and heavy expediences. It all feels very inevitable – like the spring following winter. – I was thinking of the little furry creatures in holes with their mates. How little my frocks and trunks seem to matter and being called Mrs.

September 22nd, 8 a.m. I feel this morning that my deepest reflexions aren't worth committing to paper! I have been down to fetch my letters and feel it's like the thrill of opening one's stocking on Christmas morning.

October 10th. We shall arrive in New York sometime tomorrow morning. Last night there was a moon over the sea and clouds, so that fields of silvery whiteness showed unexpectedly far away in the distance. We steamed steadily through a quiet sea, with a gentle hissing from the margin of white foam swirling past the hull, and white foam from the bow wave widening out to sea, the water dark between the whiteness. This isn't just an attempt to describe the picturesque. It's my first realization of the sea, its spaces and the depths below us where queer things grow and swim silently. I saw our funny little desires and lusts against the background of this endless sea and gloried in realizing things so overwhelming of myself. . . . It was almost the same when D. and I lay together this morning. We became conductors for some terrific current of life and here in this little cabin is the centre of an immense reality. . . . This business of going to America seems a very much bigger undertaking than I had imagined – five days away is an immense distance.

October 14th. To-morrow we move into our first room together. I have realized this morning for the first time a new sense of power, power to enfold and protect with a wide calmness – a sea of life in me.

November 8th. I don't feel very much like writing down my soul's adventures. In fact I don't feel a bit soulful to-day. But I do want to get on with this job a bit, to get down to brass tacks. . . . Two week-ends ago we went to stay in a farm-house amongst woods on the edge of a creek, at a place in Connecticut. The leaves were blazing, the air was still, our hosts were most charming and everything was intriguing, yet all the time I wanted something, wanted to make something. . . . I felt ill almost with restlessness and could find no contentment in the autumn colours. There came into my head 'ever I knew me beauty's eremite, girt with a thirsty solitude of soul', but I thought that it was nothing so aristocratic which troubled me. I thought then that it was desire for a child. My daydreams are nearly all of country cottages, of little gardens, of 'settling down' with flowers in vases and coloured curtains. I don't think of backaches, dish washing.

I want to live amongst things that grow, not amongst machines. To live in a regular rhythm with sun and rain and wind and fresh air and the coming and going of the seasons. I want a few friends that I may learn to know and understand and talk to without embarrassment or doubt.

I want to write books, to see them printed and bound.

And to get clearer ideas on this great tangle of human behaviour.

To simplify my environment so that a vacillating will is kept in the ways that I love. Instead of pulled this way and that in response to the suggestion of the crowd and the line of least resistance.

*

When seeing films of savage ritual dances I envy their intense precision and preoccupation.

Often I envy artists, musicians, dancers. . . . I think, though I'm not quite sure, that it's because they do one thing well, they show a mastery of technique – no, it's not that only – I think it's the play aspect. I don't know – precision, colour, symbolism, the language of imagination, the freedom of the spirit, the

criteria of what they do is impulse, not utility – freedom from
utility, from reality? fantasy, lure of folk tales, yet there's a precision of the imagination that these people are aiming at even
though failing often. It's not in the films, at least hardly ever,
it's in music . . . a description, a simplification and precision, a
clarifying concentration – the flight of gulls at Rye.

Also I envy the vagabond whose law is the dictates of his own
whim. Such is the lunatic though. Is this again the protest
against reality? Here I think is a very great uncertainty, the
lunatic prefers the reality of his thought to the reality of fact.
He will not compromise, he is 'all or none' in this matter. Yet
he is not all wrong, for surely thought has a reality of its own –
but only when it is based on fact. What does this mean? If I say
I am the Queen of England obviously this is thought which is
not based on fact however much I feel like the Queen of England. . . . I am trying to get at a reality of the imagination.
What about a picture – the expression of a thought – that refers
to no external facts, that is unrealistic and that has yet a truth
and reality of its own, this reality being judged only by subjective feeling. Yet it was subjective feeling that made me convinced I was the Queen of England.

The vagabond is not free from the bond of fact, he is free only
from conventional bonds, social demands, he has no sense of
'ought'. What 'oughts' do I feel now?

I ought to write more letters (etc., etc., etc.) . . .

Here followed two pages of 'oughts', mostly petty social
obligations. Then the record continues:

I think the vagabond has no 'oughts'. He has given up minding what people think of him – most of my 'oughts' were that –
and his own ideal for himself is to obey his own whims.

There were other entries of the same kind, about this
time, attempted arguments in general terms; it seemed
as if I was still trying to find out what I wanted by thinking, and had not yet discovered that only when I stopped
thinking would I really know what I wanted.

There are hardly any more notes until May 16th of the
following year, written at Santa Fé.

Adobe houses of the Mexicans, low roofed, of sun-baked earth, clustered as if growing on the hillside. A few apple trees still in blossom; beyond, the sandy hill dotted with dark junipers and cypresses. In the crooked sandy roads stray donkeys. The women wear black shawls over their heads and I've seen them walking home from Mass. Why do I love these things so? Certainly it is the instinctive life, tilling the soil, breeding animals and children, struggling for a bare living with an unquestioning faith and dependence on religious rites. But why more interesting than the struggles of the down-and-out town worker, the nonconformist prayer meeting, or a jazz party?

Is all this love for the primitive but a result of stunting my own instinctive life?

Then a year later:

It seems rather absurd that I, who am hopelessly undomestic and have no money, should think of having children. Of course it would be a great sacrifice of all the things I love, freedom, time to myself, time to wander, tramping round Europe, no responsibility. . . . Will I feel out of it when I see the country folk, with kitchen dank with drying nappies, while there's sun on fields and sea? Will I feel out of it when I see the swarming kids in tenement backyards?

*

I have given selections from my diary, trying to make them as representative as possible, in order to give an idea of the raw material from which my enterprise began. I have said that the results of keeping this record were not what I had intended. I had not found that it enabled me to balance up the facts of my life and decide what to do about it; it had only enabled me to see more facts and given me the sense that the more I wrote the more I should see. I think I must have had a dim knowledge that the act of seeing was more important to me than what I saw, since I never read through what I had written and never opened my note-book again for a year after. And when I did come to look at it I did not know what to do with it, because for me there were two separate things; on the one hand my own day-to-day experience, which was just a vague chaos, and on the other, theories about life, philosophy. I did not know how to link the two together, I did not know how to give concrete reality to the theories by examples from what I knew, or how to make the theories illuminate the facts so that I could see more by knowing where to look.*

*Because of this, the chronological sequence of the discoveries described in this book may be rather difficult to follow. Sometimes the meaning of an experience would only begin to dawn on me years afterwards, and even then I often had to go over the same ground again and again, with intervals of years between. In fact, I came to the conclusion that the growth of understanding follows an ascending spiral rather than a straight line.

CHAPTER III

Exploring the Hinterland

... I saw abundance of fowls, but knew not their kinds, neither, when I killed them, could I tell what was fit for food, and what not. At my coming back, I shot a great bird, which I saw sitting upon a tree, on the side of a large wood. I believe it was the first gun that had been fired there since the creation of the world. I had no sooner fired, but from all the parts of the wood there arose an extraordinary number of fowls, of many sorts, making a confused screaming and crying, every one according to his usual note; but not one of them of any kind that I knew. As for that creature I killed, I took it to be a kind of a hawk, its colour and beak resembling it, but it had no talons or claws more than common: its flesh was carrion and fit for nothing.

DANIEL DEFOE

DIARY-KEEPING had not brought me as far on my way as I had hoped. But if I had not been able to make myself clear about the facts of my life I had at least become more aware of my own ignorance. The more I had tried to find the facts the more I had become convinced that my own mind was something quite unknown to me. I decided therefore that my most urgent need was to become more familiar with its habits. And since it was my own mind I needed to understand, not mind in general, I did not search in books, but began to try and observe what happened when I wrote my thoughts freely without any attempt to control their direction.

I had plenty of material to work upon, from the days before I began my diary, when I had often tried to escape from worry and boredom by writing down my thoughts. I now went over these records and found that I had once tried to make a list of all the things I liked or hated, in the order in which they came into my mind.

Things I hate

Things that are meaningless and full of detail.

Suburban roads and houses.

Lace curtains.

Being ignored.

Fussy dresses.

Making a fool of myself.

Being laughed at.

Being in disagreement with people.

Being disapproved of.

Glaring lights, unshaded.

Being copied in my attempts to be original.

Being made to feel conspicuous.

Old society ladies.

Frittering time on household necessities especially when it's fine.

Spending a lot of money on something I don't like.

Being cold, having wet feet.

Being conspicuous, having arguments in public places or being unsuitably dressed.

Having my taste or actions criticized.

Quarrels between my friends.

People taking it for granted that they can share my things.

Being made use of.

Earnest, dowdy or arty women.

Pompous men.

Velvet and plush chairs.

The suggestion or feeling that you are dominated by anyone.

Hearing about the good times anyone is having if you consider those people your equals or inferiors in general.

Things I love

Flowers, light and colours.

The patience of cart-horses.

The abandon and moods of dogs.

Sharing an idea in conversation when minds move together.

Bodily sensations, hot sun, wind, rhythm, relaxation after exercise, water and fire.

The sense of strangers' moods arising from a glimpse of their faces and attitudes.

Confidences from people – strangers or friends.
Companionably sharing things, forestalling someone's need.
Getting at what someone is driving at in a play or picture.
Fairs, loitering in a crowd.
Beginning nice things.
Old implements.
Traditional knowledge for tilling the soil, seamanship and
  crafts: as opposed to efficiency methods.
Intricate mechanisms that are not man made.
Freedom from possessions.
Buying things.
Good food.
Laughing.
Hands and human skin.
Attraction towards a person.
A new idea when first it is grasped.
People singing out of doors.
Clean clothes.

Of course these lists were very incomplete: they only
represented all that I was aware of at one particular
moment. And I could not see that they had brought me
much further, for I did not yet understand that every
attempt to formulate desires, however incoherent, is a
step forward.

Then I had tried to write, not just the things I wanted
or liked, but whatever came into my head. This I had found
difficult at first, because I was obsessed by the feeling
that it was no use, that if I did not guide my thought it
was just waste of time. Here is what I found I had written
at the first attempt:

There's W. snipping things in the garden and a chaffinch
chirping that sad breeding note that reminds me of Peatfield
and spring evenings and almond blossom, then of B. and fat
buds the day after and green buds on the bush close by and – I
hope no one will find this. Why should I mind if they do? Because it seems sentimental and they might laugh. Now I'm
stuck – that being kissed and the blank feeling afterwards –

blank – frank – why do I get rhymes? – poetry – Dad – Words-
worth – Woking – our garden – squashing a frog with my bare
foot – no, it was a toad – Dad taking my photograph – it seems
this is not much use, I'm not getting far – just as I feel all sorts
of things I'm doing are not worth while – Now it's Micky [our
dog] and the time he had fits before he died and the cold stiff
feeling of touching him dead.

*

master – mother – M – Mary – maddening – mad dog –
music – much of a muchness – Alice – D – the whistle – C'.s
laughed at it – Micky, who hated being laughed at – the dog-
fight in the road – M. P., who lied and pinched me at school –
swallowing the pink pencil – lying about it – cheating over
spelling 'simple' and 'compound' – the misery of fear at being
late for school, or not knowing one's dictation – having a tooth
out – Mr C. H. – the pheasant, and I said 'Look at my baby!'
and they scolded me, just as they did when I said Mother might
have one because they said she was getting fat ... (and so on
over two more pages, ending up with): Why should my
thoughts be all memories – what about present experiences? –
again the feeling of drabness and mediocrity in my life – that
I'm no use, damned, not a person to be admired, not excelling,
hence a sort of empty futility.

On reading this through I was once more surprised to
find how different my thoughts were from what I had
expected. If anyone had said, 'A penny for your thoughts!'
when I was gazing idly out of the window or darning my
stockings, not deliberately thinking of anything, I would
have said I was vaguely noticing the sights and sounds
around me, casually going over what I intended to do,
what so and so had just said, whether it was not time for
lunch, whether there would be a letter for me. In fact
I had the impression that the mind when left to its
own devices concerned itself mainly with current affairs.
But now, when I had written my thoughts instead of
merely thinking them, only the first sentence or two were

concerned with the present and then I had plunged into memories of fifteen or twenty years ago, memories of things I had not consciously thought of for all those years, memories that I never knew I had remembered. I tried repeating the experiment and every time I did so the same thing happened. It seemed that I was normally only aware of the ripples on the surface of my mind, but the act of writing a thought was a plunge which at once took me into a different element where the past was intensely alive.

Although my glimpses of the inhabitants of these deeper waters of the mind were rather disquieting, suggesting creatures whose ways I did not know, I had found the act of writing curiously calming, so that I had gradually come to use it whenever I was over-burdened with worry. For instance, beginning with the thought of fear I had once written:

I remember telling a lie at school when I'd cheated with my poetry-book under the desk and a girl saw it. I remember making excuses to Miss B. for bad work – why did I lie? – to escape something? – what? – punishment? – what sort? – hole in corner – Death? – why death? – what does death mean? – End – anger – hate – father – cruel – home-coming – futile – foolish – who? – me? – because stupid . . . (and so on, ending up with): crying when I went to bed at B. because I was missing things – out of it – outcast – dead – ? – ? – crying at getting lost at B. – emptiness – not knowing where to turn – crying at the Tinder Box cat – fear of the white-faced Miss W. who did the ghost in the play – fear of thunder – apprehension – the before-sleeping sensations – of what? immense bigness.

Although I found many records of this kind it was difficult to understand what they might mean. So I decided to try some further experiments. Instead of letting my thoughts go their own way from the feeling of fear, I tried making a list of what I was afraid of at the present moment.

I am afraid:

– of being spoken to in the streets – I want to hide.

– that people we have social introductions to will think we do not know how to behave.

– that we will make a *faux pas*, forfeit their good opinion.

– that I'll go into a restaurant not meant for women or something like that and get stared at.

– that I'll be conspicuous.

Also, feeling a heavy burden of anxiety in my daily affairs, I tried to make a note of all my anxious moments in a single day. I wrote:

– I dithered on the pavement before crossing the street.

– I was afraid asking for information from a tram conductor, but the answer is so brusque and hurried and American that I cannot understand it.

– I was afraid to go along the day coach (in the train) to the women's toilet, past rows of people.

– I was anxious in my attitude to hotel proprietors because of doubt as to how much they'd make the bill run up.

– I tried to run the gauntlet of porters and bell-boys without having my bags wrested from me with the ensuing necessity for tips.

– I liked the comfort of a cafeteria because there's no overshadowing need to tip with doubts as to how much.

Again I was a little surprised, for I wondered why my fears, which sometimes felt like a heavy weight upon me, were so much too big for the kind of situations which appeared to arouse them. Also there seemed to be some discrepancy between the two versions of their causes. When I tried to think about them they appeared due to petty social difficulties, when I gave up thinking and just let my mind roam, I became at once preoccupied with childhood affairs and echoes of intense emotional urgency. I seemed to have two quite different selves, one which answered when I thought deliberately, another which answered when I let my thought be automatic. I decided to investigate further the opinions of the automatic one, to ask it questions and write answers without stopping to think.

So one day when I was feeling particularly under a cloud of apparently causeless anxiety I wrote:

Why this uneasiness? foreboding ? – doing wrong – punishment – that I'll be found out – I call it selfishness – I feel I'm missing something and always feel it's not for me to do the things for other people, but when I do then very often I'm happy . . . a woman's breasts – a bird's nest, all soft and smooth. feathers – the little white underneath parts of a dormouse. What's this got to do with now?

and so on, ending up with:

a black man holding you, a baby, in his arms, up in a tree – black man – father – he must have nursed me as a baby – I remember his study with the sparking coil and his singing me to sleep – 'Now the day is over'.

Although I could not then tell what all this meant, it was clear that my automatic self was busy with happenings in my remote past and was perhaps bringing over into my present concerns emotions which had no real connexion with adult life. Certainly I had not seen the electrical machine in my father's study since before I was three years old. What connexion this had with my present anxieties I could not see.

It next occurred to me to study my dreams in the same way. At that time I used very often to dream of the sea, of wanting to bathe and being in various ways prevented. I therefore chose the word 'sea' as a starting point.

SEA . . . mother – perhaps derived from 'mer' – feeling ashamed when they laughed at Miss R.'s and they said I'd painted the sea blue – why did I feel such accusations always unjust, a hot fighting to deny and escape – to bathe in the sea What does it mean? Deep cool green water to dive into, but often no bathing-dress and people watching and I never would bathe naked and damn the people – ? – ? – God – is that what the sea means? – lose myself – this is just maundering – fear of the sea at B. – fear to go in farther than up to my ankles. . . .

I was surprised at God coming into it. At that time if anyone had asked me what I thought about God I would have probably given a non-committal agnostic opinion, taking into account the latest fashion in science. I would have assumed that I had thus satisfactorily dealt with the question, taking it for granted that emotional troubles about it were things of the past, no doubt quite suitable during adolescence, but no concern of the twentieth-century adult. But since the word had cropped up in my free ideas about the sea, it now occurred to me that my automatic self might not hold the same views as my deliberate self, so I sat down to write freely, taking the word 'God' as starting point:

GOD . . . happiness – wrong – damnation – those who do not believe shall be damned – as soon as you are happy, enjoying yourself, something hunts you on – the hounds of heaven – you think you'll be lost – damned, if you are caught – so never stop – God is wicked, cruel – the Old Testament God, who commands whole cities to be put to the slaughter – a jealous God, visiting the sins – Oh God – what a God! – Hell – blasted, you'll be, annihilated, puffed out – pains of Hell gat hold upon me – you believed what they said and wanted to be a missionary to save your soul – Oh God, help us – be merciful unto us, miserable sinners – shall we never escape from the body of this death – grow old along with me, the best – they said you'd be raped by tramps on the grassy hills – I cried – Oh God, is it come to this – Lord save us – what from? Our own idea of thy nature – a fierce and jealous God – no wonder one is scared – Lord save us – be merciful to us – there is no health in us – of course not, if we always say so – Hell – blast – damnation – hurry – hurry – no time to waste –glorious sun – adoration – I love you more than God, the God of my learning – trees, grass, wind and sea – 'I give thanks and adore thee, God of the open air' – crawling

worms and mud – blind sea worms – white worms – intestinal
worms – enemas – beastly, hateful – menstruation – the hellish
smell of blood – the end of everything – prison – prison –
skirts – hampering – hairpins – hateful – humorous – laughter –
jokes – nasty – dirty – foul smells – sweaty bodies – a man's
healthful body – shirt open – P – vigour and happiness – freedom – damn the God of your Fathers – blasphemy – my God is
better than . . .

Here apparently I was interrupted. Not a little surprised at such effects of an ordinary Church of England
upbringing, I tried again, after an interval of three
months, in order to see whether this first effusion was not
perhaps the result of a temporary mood:

God – rod – sod – this is absurd – kill – ill – sin – suffering –
animals – sex – power – strength – love – what's the good of
this? – go on, go on, go on – God – rod – Almighty – spread
over the sky – like a coming thunderstorm – Almighty – all –
awful – loving? – ? – ? – God – God help us – Trees lashed by
the storm – 'But the Lord was not in the wind' – 'Lord' more
intimate but less personal to one than 'God' – Lord who walked
on the waters – what else does God mean? Holy – duty – a
fierce white light – try the opposite – Devil – D – Dad – down –
duty – downpour – this is rot – rot – rotting – decay – death –
Devil – Death – Duty – downpour – thunder – death – lightning – kill – evil – Hell – Sin – damnation – duty – damnation –
Devil – God – Satan – a personal villain – an Old Testament
character – Faust's Devil – Pleasure – Lust – decay – whoreson –
disease – plague – putrefaction – palsy – paralytic – G.P.I. – syph-
ilis – lust – loathsome – lonely – luxury – stop this alliteration
game . . . God help me – please God – if it please God – God is
a spirit – a spirit – spirits – gin – grog – spiritual – blue frocks and
tense voices – the maker of heaven and Earth – 'and God said
. . . let there be light . . . and there was light' – power – om-
nipotence – command – authority – the mean way he played
with Pharaoh – almost he holds you in a cage and you can't
escape – he is ruler and binding prisoning righteousness – is
he? – is he? – God said this *must* be – so said one's parents –
why, why, why, why? – I hate God – God doesn't want me to
be happy – '*Why* must I do it?' – 'Because I say so' – and who

are you? – why should I obey you? – I won't, I won't, I won't –
child – there's no question of obedience to laws – it's doing it
because you love it – love, love, like the moments of joy in
people and beauty and shape – then you *know* unalterably –
'before I spake as a child – understood as a child – now face to
face' – love – love is of God.

Once more I tried, this time six months later. I had
not read through what I had written on the two previous
occasions and could not remember at all what I had put.
This time, however, I did not begin with the word God,
but with the phrase 'I believe'.

I BELIEVE . . . in God, etc. – that's no use – God – something large up in the sky rather like a canopy – and a shrinking
fear inside me – memory of pain, when I have said: 'Oh God',
the ache of foreboding and fear of consequences – dread – when
I have said: 'God help me' – 'God, let me not be late for
school' – panic, terror – unreasoning, in which only God can
help – it's terror of wrong-doing, of disapproval – it seems a long
time since I felt it. God – a far-away altar to a man god –
Abraham on the mountain – the God of Moses with piercing
eyes that burnt one's face – no, it was a burning light, the face
of God, that blinded one – St Paul was also blinded – and God,
no, the Lord, was not in the Fire – yet I feel he is very much
fire – the queer awe and terror and excitement of watching a
heath fire and fighting it – the living fury of the flames – this is
as God – fierce, destructive, beautiful, inhuman – the sun also
blinds one – I cannot look upon his face – he is joyful and
strong and aloof – Balder the beautiful – the light of his
countenance is new life in one's limbs – but he is far away, be-
nign, and not a force to be feared and wondered at, as the
Fire – Fire – a queer thing sometimes glowing inside oneself –
sometimes a little flickering flame – God – the woods and
forests stand aloof – great beeches on the Downs with a brooding life of their own – rain, persistent, uncontrollable, wind –
sometimes malevolent, howling, furious seas, personal but inhuman – having purposes, apart from men's little affairs – a
vast brooding existence – more than a mass of water – the
Earth, a gentler being, passive, bearing fruit, more man's slave

than the sea and the wind and the fire – when these are tamed it is more on sufferance.

All this puzzled me a great deal. I thought – 'What is the good of imagining I accept what the scientists are saying about the nature of the universe if all the time part of myself is believing something quite different?'

Might not these apparent beliefs of my automatic self, although I had no notion of their existence, possess the power to influence my feelings and actions? And was it not important that I should find out how to control the beliefs of this part of myself, since they seemed to take so little account of what my deliberate self thought?

One day I showed some of these outpourings to a friend. We had been children together, often living in the same house, and had had exactly the same religious teaching. She said, 'But where on earth do you get such ideas! *I* never think like that!' But I said, 'Nor do I. If you had asked me what I think about I couldn't have told you a word of all that. It was only when I let my thought run on absolutely freely in writing that I discovered such thoughts. Perhaps you have another mind too which has ideas that you've never guessed at.' She said, 'Perhaps', but did not seem inclined to try the experiment.

But, for myself, I could not let the matter rest there. For this discrepancy between the views of my deliberate and automatic selves gave me an idea of what might be the reason why I found it so difficult to make up my mind what I liked or what I thought about a thing. For as a rule I had tried to make decisions without stopping to hear what my automatic self had to say, assuming that my deliberate opinions were all that mattered or even all that existed. So my decisions were made on a basis of only part of the facts, with the result that I never felt quite sure of my conclusions and was liable to reverse them on the slightest provocation. Dimly realizing this, I began to use this free writing of my thoughts as a means for making important decisions. For instance, in trying to make up my mind about a person who half attracted, half repelled me, I wrote:

I have to find out what S. stands for – rake – ruth – looking out for trouble – that's F.'s theory – there's a laugh, it sounded like a drunken man outside in the street – street girls – again what does S. mean? Smooth dark hair, golden skin like the earth of Provence – old things – wine and sunshine – my little black doll, not Omslopagas, but an older one that I lost at Campden Hill Road, with a brown body, a woolly dark head – H.'s hair – the wig in our dressing-up box – S. dresses up – Dad they said could dress up, when he came in as an Emperor – Nero – the rake who fiddled while Rome burned – fiddled . . . forbidden – Pluto – devilish – glorious sin – I've felt about it – exultation, triumph.

This, though perhaps not very intelligible to anyone else, was sufficient to show me that my emotion was concerned less with the person in question than with the irrelevant ideas which he chanced to arouse.

It was by experiments such as these that I gradually came to realize, first the existence and later the nature of this part of myself which I have called automatic. Also it seemed to me that perhaps my previous ignorance of the ways of this self might be sufficient reason why I had felt my life to be of a dull dead-level mediocrity, with the sense of real and vital things going on round the corner, out in the streets, in other people's lives. For I had taken the surface ripples for all there was, when actually happenings of vital importance to me had been going on, not somewhere away from me, but just underneath the calm surface of my own mind. Though some of these discoveries were not entirely pleasant, bringing with them echoes of terror and despair, at least they gave me a sense of being alive.

CHAPTER IV

The Coming and Going of Delight

Those that are much abroad on evenings after it is dark, in spring or summer, frequently hear a nocturnal bird passing by on the wing, and repeating often a short quick note. . . . Some of them pass over or near my house almost every evening after it is dark, from the uplands of the hill and North Fields, away down towards Dorton, where, among the streams and meadows, they find a greater plenty of food.

GILBERT WHITE

HAVING discovered that the facts of my experience were an ever-receding horizon, and that my mind had a host of thoughts I never knew about, I felt a little overwhelmed with the difficulties of my enterprise. I therefore decided that it might make the problem more manageable if I were to choose some special kind of experience and try to study that in detail. Just as in my diary I had tried to record each day's best moments, so I now set out to observe these moments more carefully, to find out what might be their cause. The first thing I noticed was that in certain moods the very simplest things, even the glint of electric light on the water in my bath, gave me the most intense delight, while in others I seemed to be blind, unresponding and shut off, so that music I had loved, a spring day or the company of my friends, gave me no contentment. I therefore decided to try to find what these moods depended upon. Could I control them myself? It did seem to me sometimes that they had been influenced by a deliberate act of mine. Particularly was I struck by the effect of writing things down. It was as if I were trying to catch something and the written word provided a net which for a moment entangled a shadowy form which was other than the meaning of the words. Sometimes it seemed that the act of writing was fuel on glowing embers, making flames leap up and throw light on the surrounding gloom, giving me fitful gleams of what was before unguessed at.

Not only did I find that trying to describe my experience enhanced the quality of it, but also this effort to describe had made me more observant of the small movements of the mind. So now I began to discover that there were a multitude of ways of perceiving, ways that were controllable by what I can only describe as an internal gesture of the mind. It was as if one's self-awareness had a central point of intensest being, the very core of one's I-ness. And this core of being could, I now discovered, be moved about at will; but to explain just how it is done to someone who has never felt it for himself is like trying to explain how to move one's ears.

Usually this centre of awareness seemed to be somewhere in my head. But gradually I found that I could if I chose push it out into different parts of my body or even outside myself altogether. Once on a night journey in a train when I could not sleep for the crowd of day impressions which raced through my head, I happened to 'feel myself' down into my heart and immediately my mind was so stilled that in a few moments I fell into peaceful sleep. But it surprised me to think that I had lived for twenty-five years without ever discovering that such an internal placing of awareness was possible.

The first hint that I really had the power to control the *way* I looked at things happened in connexion with music. Always before, my listening had been too much bothered by the haunting idea that there was far more in it than I was hearing; but occasionally I would find that I had slipped through this barrier to a delight that was enough in itself, in which I forgot my own inadequacy. But this was rare, and most often I would listen intently for a while and then find I had become distracted and was absorbed in the chatter of my own thoughts, personal preoccupations. Impatiently I would shake myself, resolving to attend in earnest for the rest of the concert, only to find that I could not lose myself by mere resolution. Gradually I found, however, that though I could not listen by direct trying I could make some sort of internal gesture after which listening just happened. I described this effort to myself in various ways. Sometimes I seemed to put my awareness into the soles of my feet, sometimes to send something which was myself out into the hall, or to feel as if I were standing just beside the orchestra. I even tried to draw a little picture to remind myself of how it felt.

In my notes I find:

Last Wednesday I went to the opera at Covent Garden, *Rigoletto*. I was dead tired and could not listen at first (sitting on the miserably cramped gallery benches), but then I remembered to put myself out of myself, close to the music – and sometimes it closed over my head, and I came away rested in feeling light-limbed.

At this time also I began to surmise that there might be different ways of looking as well as of listening.

One day I was idly watching some gulls as they soared high overhead. I was not interested, for I recognized them as 'just gulls', and vaguely watched first one and then another. Then all at once something seemed to have opened. My idle boredom with the familiar became a deep-breathing peace and delight, and my whole attention was gripped by the pattern and rhythm of their flight, their slow sailing which had become a quiet dance.

In trying to observe what had happened I had the idea that my awareness had somehow widened, that I was feeling what I saw as well as thinking what I saw. But I did not know how to make myself feel as well as think, and it was not till three months later that it occurred to me to apply to looking the trick I had discovered in listening. This happened when I had been thinking of how much I longed to learn the way to get outside my own skin in the daily affairs of life, and feel how other people felt; but I did not know how to begin. I then remembered my trick with music and began to try 'putting myself out' into one of the chairs in the room (I was alone so thought a chair would do to begin with). At once the chair seemed to take on a new reality, I 'felt' its proportions and could say at once whether I liked its shape. This then, I thought, might be the secret of looking, and could be applied to knowing what one liked. My ordinary way of looking at things seemed to be from my head, as if it were a tower in which I kept myself shut up, only looking out of the windows to watch what was going on. Now I seemed to be discovering that I could if I liked go down outside, go down and make myself part of what was happening, and only so could I experience certain things which could not be seen from the detached height of the tower. . . . One might have thought that after the discovery of such a new possibility I would have been continually coming down to look at things. Actually, however, with the press of a daily work which demanded thought, not feeling, I seem to have forgotten the fact of this new freedom, also I think I was afraid of it and loth to leave the security of my tower too often.

In these ways I began to understand that my powers of perceiving could be altered, not by directly trying to look, or trying to listen, but by this special internal gesture.

I then began to guess that not only perceiving, but doing also could be controlled in the same way. I find in my diary: 'The secret of playing ping-pong is to do it with a loose arm, relaxed.' A similar statement can be found, I should imagine, in almost any handbook on any athletic sport, but to admit its truth because everyone says so, and to prove it in one's own muscles are two very different matters. I could not believe when I first began to play that the placing of such an exuberant ball with a tiny bat could be accomplished without effort. For I had been brought up to believe that to try was the only way to overcome difficulty. ('Oh, Miss Smith, this sum is too difficult.' – 'Well, dear, just try it.') And trying meant frowning, tightening muscles, effort. So if ping-pong was difficult, one must try. The result was a stiff body, full of effort, and a jerky swipe at the ball, until someone said: 'Play with a loose arm', and I tried, unbelieving. At once the ball went crisply skimming the net to the far court, not once only, but again and again, as long as I could hold myself back from meddling. What surprised me was that my arm seemed to know what to do by itself, it was able to make the right judgements of strength and direction quite without my help. Here the internal gesture required seemed to be to stand aside.

My next discovery about movement was while darning stockings. I was usually clumsy-fingered, fumbling and impatient to be finished, but slow because I did not find the task interesting enough to keep me from day-dreaming. But one day I read somewhere that one should learn to become aware of all one's bodily movements. I did not remember what else was in the book but this struck me as interesting and I decided to try. I found I could make some internal act while darning my stocking, an act of detachment by which I stood aside from my hand, did not interfere with it, but left it to put in the needle by itself. At first I found great difficulty in restraining my head from trying to do my hand's work for it, but whenever I succeeded the results startled me; for at once there came a sense of ease and I was able to work at maximum speed without any effort. I found it was not just a momentary effect, but it returned whenever I again managed to hold my interfering brain in leash. Henceforth sewing was something to look forward to, a time to enjoy the feel of movement in my hand instead of a tiresome task to be avoided as often as possible.

Although I felt that this discovery was very important to me, I did not seem able to make use of it in the way I had hoped. Although I knew what to do I hardly ever remembered to do it, like the heroes in fairy tales who used to exasperate me by forgetting to use the charm they had been expressly given. But when I did remember to do it, I was reminded of that little one-celled animal which can spread part of its own essence to flow round and envelop within itself whatever it wants for food. This spreading of some vital essence of myself was a new gesture, more diffuse than the placing of awareness beyond myself which I had tried with music; it was more like a spreading of invisible sentient feelers, as a sea anemone spreads wide its feathery fingers. Also I saw now that my usual attitude to the world was a contracted one, like the sea anemone when disturbed by a rough touch, like an amoeba shut within protective walls of its own making. I was yet to learn that state of confidence in which my feelers would always be spread whenever I wanted to perceive.

Whether it was something in the spring weather that next reminded me of this mental gesture I cannot tell. It was nearly a year later, an April heat wave in Richmond, Virginia. One evening I saw that the half-opened leaves of trees by the dusty roadside, sycamores perhaps, made a pattern against the pale sky, like tracery of old iron-work gates or the decorations on ancient manuscripts. I had an aching desire to possess the pattern, somehow to make it mine – perhaps drawing would capture it. But I was too busy to draw and did not know how to begin even had there been time. Then I remembered to spread the arms of my awareness towards the trees, letting myself flow round them and feed on the delicacy of their patterns till their intricacies became part of my being and I had no more need to capture them on paper. The quality of the delight that followed is forgotten but I find a lame attempt to make a note of it: 'Gosh, I feel there's a bird singing high in the tree-tops inside me'. This was the nearest memory I could find of my delight, yet it had a too familiar ring and I was uneasy lest it was not truly my own expression, vaguely suspicious that someone else had said it before me.

After this I discovered another gesture, simply to press my awareness out against the limits of my body till there was vitality in all my limbs and I felt smooth and rounded. This time I tried a more mundane description and called it simply: 'That fat feeling.' Later I find a note: 'That fat feeling deepens one's breathing.' This interested me, particularly as it was another example of a bodily effect following what I have called a purely mental gesture. Also I was not long in finding uses for the 'fat feeling', for once, when returning exhausted from a day of difficult conversations, I remembered to try the pressing out gesture and after a little time found myself completely refreshed, able to respond without flagging to the demands of the evening.

A little later I found a first clue as to what was preventing me spreading my feelers whenever I needed. It was one evening when I was trying to feel out in this way while watching the players at the Chinese Theatre in New York; since there were no intelligible words to engage my attention, I was finding it difficult to keep my thoughts from wandering back to the day's preoccupations which I wished to forget. I thought how much there was of entrancing interest going on before me if I only could reach it, and how petty and nagging were the anxieties of the day which continually distracted me. I had therefore tried deliberately to spread my feelers. No sooner had I made the gesture, however, than I became aware of a vague panic in the back of my mind prompting me to withdraw again into myself like a frightened spider who tucks in his legs, shamming dead.

All these experiences seemed to follow some special internal act, and my next discovery was that this act could be towards inactivity, a letting go. One day I was sitting in the sun alone on a ship's deck with the sea all about me and a gentle wind. I was restless and unhappy, worried because I seemed cut off from enjoying something which I had so often longed for in dark days of winter and cities. I knew that I ought to be happy now that I was having what I wanted, sun and leisure and sea. Suddenly I noticed that I was trying to think, and that I seemed to have taken it for granted that I would be happy if only I could think of something. Not that I had any special problem that needed solving at that particular moment, it was simply the feeling that one ought to have thoughts, ideas, something interesting to say about all one had seen and heard. But with the sun and the wind and the good food I was too turnip-headed to think, my body simply wanted to do nothing. Of course as soon as I became aware of this idea that one ought to have thoughts I realized how silly it was and I stopped trying to do anything, I simply 'let go'. At once the whiteness of sun-lit ropes against the sea leapt to my eyes and I was deeply content to sit and look.

I also found another example of the effects of passivity. I had always been vaguely interested in pictures, but worried because so often I could not say what I liked; I never seemed to know how to decide, except on a few occasions when a picture would seem to leap at me before I had begun to look at it, when I was still busy about something else. But one day I stopped in front of a Cézanne still-life – green apples, a white plate and a cloth. Being tired, restless, and distracted by the stream of bored Sunday afternoon sight-seers drifting through the galleries, I simply sat and looked, too inert to remember whether I ought to like it or not. Slowly then I became aware that something was pulling me out of my vacant stare and the colours were coming alive, gripping my gaze till I was soaking myself in their vitality. Gradually a great delight filled me, dispelling all boredom and doubts about what I ought to like. . . . Yet it had all happened by just sitting still and waiting. If I had merely given a cursory glance, said: 'Isn't that a nice Cézanne?' and drifted on with the crowd, always urged to the next thing, I would have missed it all. And also if I had not been too tired to think I would have said: 'Here is a Cézanne, here is something one ought to like', and I would have stood there trying to like it but becoming less and less sure what I felt about it. I am reminded in writing this of another experience during fatigue, when I was too tired to think. One midsummer morning, after dancing so late that it did not seem worth while going to bed, I had walked out alone on Hampstead Heath in the bright sunlight and lain on my back amongst the bracken watching the slow march of clouds. At once I had slipped Into such a happiness as I had never known till then, for this was in the days before I had begun to watch for delights and how they came.

In the next striking experience that occurred to me I perceived a new quality. We had just returned to England after two years away, and, landing at Plymouth, were meandering across Cornwall in a Sunday train which every few miles slowed up and creaked to stillness in the quiet of a village station. At first I was deep in my own thoughts, only glancing out of the window occasionally with a sense of the utter familiarity of the country and faintly disappointed that I was feeling no great emotion of home-coming, for it all seemed a little obvious and ordinary. As so often before, my emotions were failing to live up to a romantic moment. Then something happened. Perhaps I remembered to spread myself, to feel out into the landscape. I do not remember the precise gesture. But suddenly I began to notice white cottages and lanes and tidy green fields, and something, either the colours or the shapes, or the character of the land, aroused such a deep resonance in me that I sat, as if meeting a lover, aglow with an almost unbearable delight.

At this time, remembering the vague sense of panic I had observed in the Chinese Theatre, I gradually became aware of something which seemed to be preventing me making these gestures of feeling out. Certain fears began to take form, shadowy and elusive as yet, but intense as a missed heart-beat. Chiefly there seemed to be a fear of losing myself, of being overtaken by something. One day I was lying half asleep on the sands when I saw a gull alight quite close to me, with wings stretched above its back in that fashion peculiar to great winged birds when they settle on the ground. Without thinking, I felt myself into its movement with a panic ecstasy and then turned quickly round upon my fear, for the first time framing the question: 'What is this ogre which tries to prevent me from feeling the reality of things?' But I was too slow, it had vanished before I could recognize its shape.

I did not find out anything more about control of mood for another year and did not progress very far in applying what I had already learnt. Then one day, when on a holiday in the Black Forest in Germany, I discovered a more vivid power of perceiving than ever before. The weather was wet and cold, my companion was nervously ill so that we were prevented from following our plan of a walking tour, and, being unable to speak German, I had little wherewith to distract either of us from depressed brooding. I was lonely and filled with a sense of inadequacy, I longed to do something, to act, as an alternative to the ceaseless chatter of worrying thoughts, I was angry with my companion for being ill and angry with myself for being so self-centred as to grumble. I felt cramped that we must stay in a town, and my only delight was when the cold night air, blowing down empty streets, brought the smell of encircling forest. I said: 'If only the sun would come out then I could rest without thinking'. And one morning I woke to find that the sun was out, and I went into the forest, wandering up a path to a cottage where they served drinks on little tables under apple trees, overlooking a wide valley. I sat down and remembered how I had sometimes found changes of mood follow when I tried to describe in words what I was looking at. So I said: 'I see a white house with red geraniums and I hear a child crooning'. And this most simple incantation seemed to open a door between me and the world. Afterwards, I tried to write down what had happened:

. . . Those flickering leaf-shadows playing over the heap of cut grass. It is fresh scythed. The shadows are blue or green, I don't know which, but I feel them in my bones. Down into the shadows of the gully, across it through glistening space, space that hangs suspended filling the gully, so that little sounds wander there, lose themselves and are drowned; beyond, there's a splash of sunlight leaping out against the darkness of forest, the gold in it flows richly in my eyes, flows through my brain in still pools of light. That pine, my eye is led up and down the straightness of its trunk, my muscles feel its roots spreading wide to hold it so upright against the hill. The air is full of sounds, sighs of wind in the trees, sighs which fade back into the overhanging silence. A bee passes, a golden ripple in the quiet air. A chicken at my feet fussily crunches a blade of grass. . . .

I sat motionless, draining sensation to its depths, wave after wave of delight flowing through every cell in my body. My attention flickered from one delight to the next like a butterfly, effortless, following its pleasure; sometimes it rested on a thought, a verbal comment, but these no longer made a chattering barrier between me and what I saw, they were woven into the texture of my seeing. I no longer strove to be doing something, I was deeply content with what was. At other times my different senses had often been in conflict, so that I could either look or listen but not both at once. Now hearing and sight and sense of space were all fused into one whole.

I do not know how long I sat there in absolute stillness,

watching. Eventually, I stood up, stretched and returned along the little path down the hillside, freed from my angers and discontents and overflowing with peace. But there were many questions to be answered. Which of the things I had done had been important in the awakening of my senses? Or was it nothing I had done, but some spell from the forest and the sun? Could I repeat the experience and so have a permanent retreat for the cure of my angers and self-pity? If just looking could be so satisfying, why was I always striving to have things or to get things done? Certainly I had never suspected that the key to my private reality might lie in so apparently simple a skill as the ability to let the senses roam un-fettered by purposes. I began to wonder whether eyes and ears might not have a wisdom of their own.

CHAPTER V

Searching for a Purpose

The next day I made another voyage; and now, having plundered the ship of what was portable, and fit to hand out, I began with the cables; and cutting the great cables into two pieces such as I could move, I got two cables and a haw-ser on shore, with all the iron work I could get; and having cut down the sprit-sail-yard and the mizen-yard, and every-thing I could to make a large raft, I loaded it with all those heavy goods, and came away. But my good luck began to leave me, for this raft was so unwieldy, and so overladen, that after I was entered the little cove where I had landed the rest of my goods, not being able to guide it so handily as I did the other, it overset and threw me and all my cargo into the water.

DANIEL DEFOE

In the last chapter I have tried to describe certain ex-periences which stand out in my memory as being of a different quality from my everyday perceptions. Such delights, however, were essentially solitary; I had never been able to find them when I was with other people, except in the loneliness of a crowd. But I was not content with a central point to my life which should cut me off from humanity, and I felt convinced there was more if only I could find it. I realized that the greater part of my days were spent with other people, partly by the necessi-ties of work, partly by habit, partly by choice based on a vague desire to find something in companionship which continually eluded me; but not only did I fail to find any satisfactions approaching those of my solitary moments, I also continued to suffer from those fears, anxieties and boredoms which had prompted my first setting out ,on this journey of discovery. So, during this time when I was trying to follow up and observe the habits of these strange birds of delight which I could sometimes tempt into my garden, I was also busy cultivating my own potato patch.

To follow the instructions given in a book was in a sense a reversal of my main principle, since the very aim of my enterprise was to try to observe the facts of my own life and to find out what was true for me. But at first my intention ran ahead of my capacity. Having found that it was not so easy to determine the facts, and being impatient to reach my goal as soon as possible, I was tempted by the glowing promises of the handbooks on mental training. So I went back over all the instructions that I had ever vaguely tried to follow at various times in the years before I had begun to ask what were the facts of my life.

From these books I had gathered that my chief task was to practise exercises in concentration, for they maintained that in order to adapt oneself to other people without tongue-tying self-consciousness it was necessary to control one's thoughts as the occasion might demand. This had seemed sensible enough and I had then read that the essential first step in learning to concentrate was to decide what was one's aim in life. So I had sat down cheerfully one day with a pencil and paper for this preliminary task, thinking to finish it and be ready to begin the exercises in half an hour or so. But I had found it was not so easy. The handbooks had suggested that one should want some definite achievement – to be promoted in one's business, to earn so much money, to get something done – but none of such special aims that I had been able to think of seemed sufficient to enchannel all my enthusiasms. It seemed then that every time I had tried in the previous years to gain control of my thought I had been stopped at the outset by this difficulty. There had of course been times in the past when I had actually worked for a purpose, such as, for instance, obtaining training for my professional work. Whenever I had managed to hold such a partial purpose in mind I had certainly achieved more than I had ever expected, but neither the working for a purpose nor some measure of success had brought the indirect results promised by the mental training system. I would still have had to put large ticks on their self-examination lists against: 'self-conscious', 'lacking in will-power', 'wandering attention', 'self-distrustful'. And I was still quite unable to achieve the clear all-embracing purpose which it was said would cure these defects.

Certainly when I had first looked at my activities and tried to find an underlying motive, the dominant one had seemed to be trying to please people, to keep up with what was expected of me and to avoid offending. This was despicable, I felt, but perhaps the cure for it might be a dominant aim of my own which would lead me to be independent of what other people thought? Here I remembered an incident when I had not minded what other people thought, so strong had been my own urge. It was at the Zoo when I had been looking at the desert mice in the Small Mammal House. I suddenly had the idea that I would like one as a pet (I had had a series of dormice, lizards, white rats, as a child). The keeper told me it would be possible to buy one but I must apply at the office. Being Saturday the appropriate official was away. But I was not to be put off and surprised myself by the urgency of my determination to get that mouse. With a most unusual tenacity I went ahead, overruling the opposition and natural irritation which I encountered. In the end I went home in triumph with my mouse, vaguely puzzled at having been so importunate.

It seemed then that I was not incapable of strong purpose. The problem was really how to bring such energy of desire into relation with my everyday life – I could not build my life around the possession of a desert mouse. So, giving up for the moment the attempt to find a single purpose, I looked amongst my papers and found a list I had once tried to make of *all* the things I thought I wanted. There is no date on the scrap of paper on which this is written but I think I made it before I began to keep a daily record of 'wants' in my diary. Here is the list, and I have added notes to explain what I remember was in my mind at the time:

– a perfect companion (when writing this I remembered how, as a child, although I had several very good friends, I was always looking for one who would really share my interest in birds and animals. I used to review hopefully all new children who came to live in our road).
– to be famous for some service to the race, a great pioneer work (this was in my moods of uplift).
– a great many friends.
– to achieve a unique work of art (I think I meant, paint a great picture).
– to 'plumb to the depths of human experience'.
– to be recognized as a unique individual (I wanted my separateness recognized, for I remembered how sometimes my father used to attribute to my elder sister something which I had done, confusing our names).
– to be in people's confidence (I had always felt a little out of it at school and one day when very young I was delighted because two girls I admired told me a secret. I went home singing: 'I know a secret, I know a secret').

This was all very well but I could now see why it had not brought me much further; for I had never been able to decide which one of these could be made the central purpose of my life. I could easily make lists of whatever came into my head but could not decide between them because in one mood one would be important, in a different mood another; I had never followed any one of them whole-heartedly. I had thought I wanted a great many friends, but had often refused invitations because I hated to feel the beautiful free space of an empty day, free for me to do what I liked in, broken into by social obligations. I had thought I wanted to be a unique individual, but had been filled with shame when anyone disagreed with me, hastening to take back what I had said. I had thought I wanted to be importantly useful in the world, but avoided all opportunities for responsibility. I had thought I wanted to plumb human experience to the depths, and yet had striven to remain immaculately aloof from all emotional disturbance.

One thing struck me as odd. The actual aims were expressed in adult terms but the ideas which I felt explained them were chiefly in terms of childhood memories.

Then I found the record of another attempt to define my main purpose. One Saturday afternoon (still before I had begun to write my diary) I had been walking along the Thames tow-path towards Richmond, idly watching the crews practising on the river, when it came into my head that I knew what my purpose was. Now my work at that time was such that I must seek knowledge, read books, always be trying to amass more information; and – influenced no doubt by the current emphasis on science – I had thought at times that this was also my chief purpose. For instance, once after scanning some book on the history of the suffragette movement I was filled with the glow of noble inspiration, and wrote: 'These people were epoch-makers politically ... surely the pioneers of the next advance will be dealing with the mind. Anyhow your job is the mind and to find out how it works.' At that time I was still easily stirred to noble enthusiasms. But now in the grey February afternoon by the river I had known this was not true in the sense I had meant it; for the quietness of the weather had lapped over into my mind and stilled it so that I could see clearly into myself. When I came home I had scribbled on a scrap of old paper:

I want, not knowledge, but *experience* of the laws of things; to suffer them, not only to observe them. To apprehend with regard to the things I come across – the necessities of their being, what immutable law makes them what they are, their physics and chemistry and actuality, to feel it. . . . Knowing is no good unless you feel the urgency of the thing. Maybe this is love; your being becomes part of it, giving yourself to it.

When I had written this I immediately forgot it. Several years later I remembered the sense of understanding from that afternoon but not what I had understood. And now, when I was once more deliberately looking for a purpose, I happened to find the paper and although when I read it through it did not seem to mean much, I still had the feeling that it was important. Actually it has taken me many years to understand what I wrote then, so although I think now that I was right in looking on it as a true expression of my purpose, it could not serve as a principle by which I could deliberately guide my daily affairs. Certainly it did not seem at the time that I had found an aim which would give point to the exercises in concentration.

By now I had reviewed all my past attempts to find happiness by following the instructions of mental training experts. Gradually a conclusion began to emerge. Instead of, as always before, assuming that they were right and therefore my inability to reach the promised results must be due to my own weakness, I began to ask whether this really was the way to find what I wanted. I had been continually exhorted to define my purpose in life, but I was now beginning to doubt whether life might not be too complex a thing to be kept within the bounds of a single formulated purpose, whether it would not burst its way out, or if the purpose were too strong, perhaps grow distorted like an oak whose trunk has been encircled with an iron band. I began to guess that my self's need was for an equilibrium, for sun, but not too much, for rain, but not always. I felt that it was as easily surfeited with one kind of experience as the body with one kind of food, and that it had a wisdom of its own, if only I could learn to interpret it. So I began to have an idea of my life, *not as the slow shaping of achievement to fit my preconceived purposes, but as the gradual discovery and growth of a purpose which I did not know.* I wrote: 'It will mean walking in a fog for a bit, but it's the only way which is not a presumption, forcing the self into a theory.'

It took me a long time to realize the meaning of this discovery. Although I had kept a fairly regular diary for six months, had made records of my moments of delight, had made excursions into the hinterlands of my own mind, still I did not understand what was the crux of the problem. I had even achieved several of the things I had wanted in external life; for I was married, had reached America, and had opportunity of doing the kind of work I had hoped for. Yet my thoughts were still hovering round this problem of purposes. For in New York I wrote:

I want to change my attitudes; it fills me with restlessness that I am always striving after something and I don't know what it is. I envy people, artists chiefly. I want to achieve the play attitude. By this I mean concentration in an activity which has no apparent use just for the delight of doing it. Why do I want this? I don't know quite, it just seems very desirable. Perhaps it gives freedom from this endless pursuit of one's soul's salvation . . . 'he that would save his soul'. . . . I want to lose it. . . . Play means to me freedom – freedom from fears. It is an expression of the dignity of the soul, enslaved in no bondage of justification. Perhaps then if I am to learn to play I must go down to hell and find what taskmaster is lurking there.

I walked down Fifth Avenue in the sparkling sun, impelled to be idle, but impelled to find some justification for my idleness. I was always full of purposes, always driving myself to do more things – to read more books, to learn more languages, to see more people, not to miss anything. Always I must 'get on', even amusing myself in the ordinary ways, going to night clubs, dances, was 'getting on' – 'getting on' in knowing about the ways of the world, a miser-like grabbing and piling up of experience.

I tried to reckon what I must pay to change this attitude. I wrote:

How many theatres and cinemas will I give up to think it out? Will thinking do it? How much shall I leave undone my official work for which I can receive justification? How much shall I amass fewer acquaintances? What self-idea must I throw overboard? The social self which wants everybody's approval? I think her master is a fear in hell.

Here I felt was a most praiseworthy attempt to be business-like and count the cost of my intended enterprise. The trouble was that I did not know how to answer my own questions, and though guessing that I must give up something, I could not tell where might lie the crux of the surrender. Only I had a suspicion that my constant worry over the worthwhileness of what I did was concerned with some dominating fear hidden in the dark hinterlands of thought. A little drawing, which I scribbled at the time, unknowingly, now seemed to illustrate the issues.

There is a figure on the right at the bottom who is separate from all the confusion and noise, and unable to achieve either the absorbed action of the sharp-shooter girl on horse-back or the swooning abandon of the lady

on the left. The drawing seems to show what the separated figure wants, but cannot get. Her attitude also shows the way she was trying to get it – by intense effort, determination. Although at the time the drawing meant nothing to me, I could now see it as a graphic expression of the fact that I did not know that I could only get the most out of life by giving myself up to it. The markings on the left seem to express the general clash of impulses I felt, and the horses at the bottom probably stood for feelings of unused energy within.

It seemed then that my purpose in life was to get the most out of life. And because I was not capable of more than very muddled thinking, I still assumed that the way to this was to strive to do more and more things; and this, in spite of my intuition about the need for surrender. Here then was a deadlock. I wanted to get the most out of life, but the more I tried to grasp, the more I felt that I was ever outside, missing things. At that time I could not understand at all that my real purpose might be to learn to have no purposes.

This deadlock continued for more than a year. I still kept spasmodic diary records but had no idea how to begin to make use of the experiences I recorded. Then, still exasperated by my own incapacities and sense of inadequacy, I set out yet again to learn concentration by practising exercises. Again I read in the handbook of the need to define my chief purpose and also my subordinate purposes. And again I began with a question-mark under the heading of chief purpose, for I did not remember the purpose I had found by the river, or my dim guess of the need, not to grasp, but to give up. But under 'subordinate purposes' I wrote forty items. These comprised all the things I found myself trying to do or making plans for in my leisure moments. Here is a selection:

No. 2. to have enough money to have a child.
5. to dress moderately well.
7. to know what is going on in the world.
11. to be able to talk well.
17. to get to know M. better.
21. to answer my letters.

27. to feel at ease and adequate with all the people I meet.
28. to do things because I really want to and not because other people do them or to please them.
34. to read French easily.
36. to express my feelings, be impulsive and emotional, not consistent and aloof.
38. to be able to detect and bring out the significant things in the people I meet: not miss 'so much and so much' through blindness and ego-centricity.

Then, although I still could not say what my main purpose was, a certain sense of direction began to emerge. While drifting with the crowd in the past years I had been trying to get the most out of life in quantity; it was the number of different experiences I had had which pleased me, whether I had lain by the shores of the Mediterranean, or danced in a Harlem night club, or watched the Yale-Harvard 'ball game'. When friends came and told me of things they had seen and I had not, I was downcast and felt a failure. But consideration of my store of delights was leading me to a different aim. I began to want intensity, not extensity, to look for quality, not quantity, in living. And to find this I had to learn to distinguish good quality from bad quality. So I wrote:

This is really what I want. I want to discover ways to discriminate the important things in human life. I want to find ways of getting past this blind fumbling with existence.

Gradually, and very spasmodically at first, I seem to have begun this attempt to discriminate.

Last night I was tired and things seemed colourless. . . . D. suggested finishing our game of chess after our baths, so we sat on the bed after midnight. He made me feel again that things are not what they are supposed to be, that the important things are the undefined things – as if one did not know the name of one's love, and so could never find him except by chance. It is something to do with understanding one person and their many moods, understanding their silences, the times between, the doings that have no purpose beyond themselves. R. and T. are nearer it. S. W. and P. B. make me forget it, and want exciting things to happen, flirtations, success, wide contacts.

One day I wrote:

The squares and angles of the outhouse from my window are most comforting. There's a phrase in my head, 'the texture of experience'. These are facts and more vital than the attempts to prove things. . . . What's it matter if they prove them or not? There was a boy playing in the ditch. . . . Are all these seeming 'intimations of immortality' but evasions, escapes from the struggles of life? Hell, I wish I knew!

What seemed far more important was the clatter of horses' hoofs outside echoing in the air of the first warm day.

Then came another attempt to express my main purpose:

But this is what I want. To make discoveries about human beings, to know what they are. And I suppose my trouble is that I am not convinced that intellectual study of the human being is the way to it. Maybe to be a complete human being oneself is the only way. And how does one do that?

Yet I still thought that all this was probably too vague, I should have determined on something more objective, something to be done, 'to be Prime Minister, like Disraeli, or to find out the truth about the atom'. But all such specific purposes still seemed to me to exclude something, to run the risk that if I had a preconceived idea of where I was going I might 'miss the many-splendoured thing'. I wrote:

I feel too blind, or too lacking in desire, to feel I have any overmastering purpose to force upon the world.

All the same, I thought I was clear enough now about the *sort* of thing I wanted, I thought I had formulated enough of the general direction of my purpose to make it possible to try the exercises in concentration. For it was obvious that I had so often failed to get the most out of whatever I did because my attention was always wandering to something else. So I began to try, and the result was a sense of new possibilities in richness of thought. In my ordinary way of thinking a table, for instance, only existed for me, as it affected myself; if I banged my knee against it – 'Oh, bother that table', if my back ached – 'Oh, this table is too low'. But unless it immediately concerned me I took no notice of it, for it was something too familiar to bother with. So I thought as I began this exercise that I was in for a dull time, but since my table was the nearest concrete object it would do to begin with. Now, however, almost at once, my sense of dull duty to be performed vanished, and the table began to exist in its own right.

Next time I tried a lump of coal on the hearth. From having been aware of it simply as something to burn I began to feel its blackness as a quite new sensation, to feel its 'thingness' and the thrust of its shape, to feel after its past in forests of giant vegetation, in upheavings of the land passing to eons of stillness, and then little men tunnelling, the silence and cleanliness of forests going to make up London's noisy filth.

Then I chose a small tin mug. It was an ugly object. Nevertheless I tried to keep my thoughts fixed upon it for fifteen minutes. This time I did not become concerned with its origin but simply let its form imprint itself upon my mind. Slowly I became aware of a quite new knowledge. I seemed to sense what I can only call the 'physics' of that mug. Instead of merely seeing its shape and colour I felt what I described to myself as its 'stresses and strains', the pressures of its roundness and solidity and the table holding it up. This sense did not come at once and I suppose it might never have come if I had not sat still and waited. But from this few minutes' exercise on a tin mug I had found a clue which eventually led me to understand what was the significance of many pictures, buildings, statues, which had before been meaningless.

Now concentration began to possess a quite new meaning. The word had always in the past been connected with the dull and burdensome, it was like having a purpose in life, it meant missing things, shutting out the unexpected; just as being 'good' at school meant turning from the lovely things, whipping oneself away from lazy moments in the sun and from chances of escaping the class-room into glorious loneliness. But now, concentration, instead of being a matter of time-tables and rules, was a magician's wand. By a simple self-chosen act of keeping my thoughts on one thing instead of dozens, I had found a window opening out across a new country of wide horizons and unexplored delights.

But even so, I did not continue my concentration exercises. The reason was partly, I think, that although I found them fascinating in themselves, they still did not seem to have any effect on the day-to-day boredoms and inadequacies of my life with other people.

In spite, however, of no marked immediate results following from this endeavour to learn control of my thought, the attempt to define my purpose in life had stimulated certain ideas which were to bear fruit later. I had certainly found that I was continually whipping my will to effort after endless goals, goals which might be actually shutting me away from what I really wanted. Why I felt such a desperate urge to reach these things I could not tell, but I had at least begun to guess that my greatest need might be to let go and be free from the drive after achievement – if only I dared. I had also guessed that perhaps when I had let these go, then I might be free to become aware of some other purpose that was more fundamental, not self-imposed private ambitions but some thing which grew out of the essence of one's own nature. People said: 'Oh, be *yourself* at all costs'. But I had found that it was not so easy to know just what one's self was. It was far easier to want what other people seemed to want and then imagine that the choice was one's own.

CHAPTER VI

Searching for a Rule

Do you continually curtail your effort till there be nothing
of it left? . . . By non-action there is nothing which cannot be
effected.

LAO-TZE

AT this stage I felt as though I were fiddling with the
stops and keys of a strange instrument; every now and
then some movement of mine would be followed by a
peal of sound, yet I could not be sure which one of the
things I did had produced it.

Often when I felt certain that I had discovered the
little mental act which produced the change I walked on
air, exulting that I had found the key to my garden of
delight and could slip through the door whenever I
wished. But most often when I came again the place
seemed different, the door overgrown with thorns and
my key stuck in the lock. It was as if the first time I had
said 'abracadabra' the door had opened but the next
time I must use a different word. For years I had blundered on, sometimes forgetting the door altogether, trying to content myself with external affairs. Often when I
felt inadequate I tried to make up for it by striving after
the things other people did; when I felt dull and had
nothing to say at parties I would still make resolutions to
read more books so that I would know about the things
the others were talking of. I would resolve to read the
papers every day and I tried not to miss what was going
on, I wanted to have seen the latest well-spoken-of film
or play. In buses and tubes I was always trying to think
so that I would have views about things, and be able to

hold forth as other people did, giving my opinions. But the only result seemed to be frequent weariness and a constant sense of the number of things I had to do piling up and toppling over upon me. When I stopped to think, it used to amaze me how I could for months together be caught up in the rush to get things done, how I was able to forget completely all the ways I had found of altering the quality of my experience and forget even that I had the power to alter it.

Because of the fatal easiness of this forgetting I was always, whenever I remembered and again found the door, trying to make a rule by which I would know how to find my way back. Like Hansel I was trying to find something to mark the path which would not be carried away by the birds of my external interests. Of course there had been a stage before this when I had not even realized that I needed to find any rule. For before I began to enquire into the nature of my experience I had had no idea that there was any question of how to control thoughts and behaviour. I had assumed that there was something in me called will which only had to command in order to be obeyed; that I only had to decide what I wanted, to say, 'I will do this', for it to happen. So, when I had a sudden idea of what sort of person I would like to be, I wrote it down in triumph as if the act of deciding to be it was as good as becoming it. When what I had resolved upon did not happen I thought it must be due to some inherent weakness of this thing called will in myself. It never occurred to me to question my whole idea about what this will was for.

But when resolutions had repeatedly failed me I tried, blindly and spasmodically, but still tried, to guess what was wrong. In flashes I seemed to understand the difficulty but after I had written it down I lost the idea.

All this never resting constant effort to think about some-thing that will get you on – which will make you the sort of person you want to be – is but another way of trying to escape surrender – trying to be what you are not.

But I did not understand what I had to surrender to. I wrote:

The secret of lack of concentration seems to me to be fear, guilt, a continual running away, escaping, hiding – a sense that what one is doing at the moment won't save one, but something else is better – always the thing you are not doing is going to be the only thing.

But I did not know what I was running away from. Then I saw myself as trying to hide something from a hostile world. I wrote:

What I think happens is this. Your conviction of being a miserable sinner makes you always on guard to avoid being found out, so everything you do is restrained, cautious, half-hearted, and, of course, rather a failure; which hits back and again convinces you of deficiency, of weakness and inferiority, a vicious circle.

As far as I can see the only break-away from this circle is:

(1) By convincing your automatic self that you are not a miserable sinner, that no eternal damnation is threatening you.

(2) The first is negative, driving out the devil. The positive means seems to be to direct your energies away from self – if you do not care for yourself fears for your own safety or damna-tion will lose their power.

But I did not know how to convince my automatic self or to direct my energies away from myself.

Then I began to see a connexion between the vague feeling of guilt, of inadequacy, and the intense preoccu-pation with what other people thought of me which so often made me tongue-tied for fear of saying the wrong thing. I wrote:

You may think you've accepted yourself as a fool but you

can't bear that other people should know it. Your own feeling of guilt is such that you can't take satisfaction in the truth of yourself, but only in other people's opinions.

One day I had a premonition of what I must do and was apparently feeling heroic, for I wrote:

It will be a sore fight letting go and letting the sea in.

As I have said it was only gradually that I began to grasp the nature of the problem, to understand that it was not necessarily the weakness of my effort which failed to turn the key, but the wrong movement, holding it upside down or perhaps a key which did not fit. But although I began to see that some different action was necessary, something more than the willed command, I still did not know enough what that action might be. In fact, it was only when I had begun to look through my diary and analyse it that I had come upon a clue to the problem.

Certainly I had found that my best moments, moments that I counted as successes, had not followed the toothgritting keeping of resolutions which I had been taught to believe was the only way of getting things done. But they did often follow what appeared to be a voluntary act of mine, although the act itself was almost the opposite of my idea of willing. Willing to me meant asserting myself, while what appeared to be the significant act here was almost a deliberate negation of self, an active holding back from any form of action, a keeping myself in leash, or a putting something of myself out into the object I looked at so that for the moment my own will was wiped out. Gradually now I saw more clearly what had been my assumptions about the meaning of 'trying' and 'willing'. 'Trying' was an internal clenching and grunting which I seemed to imagine had a virtue of its own; for how often had I not successfully excused my failures at school and at home by saying, 'Well, I did *try*.' Once, quite recently, when I had answered a difficult question by saying, 'I am trying to think', someone had said, 'Don't try, think.' So at long last I had grasped the idea that the indispensable preliminary to every task which appeared difficult was not a general tensing and contraction, but that the response I hoped for would happen if I just looked in the direction I wanted to go and waited.

It seemed as if I had been used to treating thought as a wayward child which must be bullied into sitting in one place and doing one thing continuously, against its natural inclination to go wandering, to pick one flower here and another there, to chase a butterfly or climb a tree. So progress in concentration had at first meant strengthening my bullying capacity. And, just as I had once wanted to teach but had given up the idea because I felt sure I had not the strength of will to force children to sit still, so now I was continually giving up in despair, convinced that I could never learn to keep my thoughts docile, keep them from going wandering in the garden. But now, as I have tried to show in the last chapter, my idea of the meaning of concentration was changing, just as my idea of the meaning of education had done. I began to see that I must play the Montessori teacher to my thought, must leave it free to follow its own laws of growth, my function being to observe its activities, provide suitable material to enchannel them, but never to coerce it into docility. Actually it was many years earlier that I first happened upon this analogy, but I could not then understand what it might mean; just as a traveller while still far off may catch one glimpse of the spires of his destination, but may not see them again until, after devious paths, he finds himself close upon them.

Before, I had assumed that there were just two attitudes, one a striving with whips to make my thoughts follow the path I had chosen, the other a witless dreaming, letting them wander off, useless and blindly nosing after grass. Now I began to think that there might be, not just two, but as many different attitudes as steps in a dance. I tried to make a list of all the different gestures which I had found effective and the situations in which I thought they would be appropriate: 'that fat feeling' when I was tired, putting myself outside myself for listening to music, and so on. I imagined myself practising each one as a dancer would first practise the separate steps and then learn to do each at the right moment, to leap or pirouette or curtsey as the music might dictate. But when I began to classify the gestures to be learnt, I found it too difficult. Also I was surprised to find how interchangeable they were. Detaching myself, holding myself apart from what I was doing, which I first learnt while darning my stockings, seemed equally effective in appreciating the landscape; music, when it seemed to be nothing but meaningless sound, would leap into significance as much when I imagined myself to be dead as when I pushed my awareness out into the hands of the conductor.

While considering these things a new idea began to emerge. It gradually dawned on me that every one of the gestures I had discovered involved a kind of mental *activity*. Whether it was the feeling of listening through the soles of my feet, or perhaps putting into words what I was seeing, each gesture was a deliberate mental act which arrested the casual drift of my thought, with results as certain as though I had laid my hand on the idly swinging tiller of a boat. It seemed to me now that it was

perhaps not *what* I did with my thought that brought the
results, but the fact that I did anything at all. Yet this
activity was as different from my usual attempts to take
control of my thoughts as steering a boat is from trying
to push it. So I began to wonder whether there were
perhaps not many gestures which I must learn in their
appropriate places, but only one which really mattered.
And perhaps this one offered a third possibility in the
control of attention, a possibility which the books had
not made clear to me at all. I must neither push my
thought nor let it drift. I must simply make an internal
gesture of standing back and watching, for it was a state
in which my will played policeman to the crowd of my
thoughts, its business being to stand there and watch
that the road might be kept free for whatever was coming. Why had no one told me that the function of will
might be to stand back, to wait, not to push? The lonely
policeman who relied on his physical strength to keep
back the crowd would soon be swept away; as my will
had constantly been by the surging thoughts.

CHAPTER VII

Two Ways of Looking

> ... and this fence was so strong that neither man nor beast could get into it, or over it. This cost me a great deal of time and labour, especially to cut the piles in the woods, bring them to the place and drive them into the earth.
>
> The entrance into this place I made to be, not by a door, but by a short ladder, to go over the top; which ladder, when I was in, I lifted over after me, and so I was completely fenced in, and fortified, as I thought, from all the world, and consequently slept secure in the night, which otherwise I could not have done, though, as it appeared afterward, there was no need of all this caution from the enemies I apprehended danger from.
>
> ₁ DANIEL DEFOE

I THOUGHT I had now found out how I could, to some extent at least, control my moments of delight. Certainly my rule did not always work, but it worked often enough to convince me that I was on the right track. So I now tried to find out what this internal act of waiting actually did to my thought.

In the first place, these sudden illuminations forced me to see that my preconceived ideas about 'thought' and 'facts' were quite inadequate. Slowly I realized that the facts were not separate things which were there for anyone to pick up, but an ever-changing pattern against a boundless background of the unknown, an immense kaleidoscope changing constantly according to the different ways you looked at it. They were not 'given' as in geometry, staying there at the top of the page while all you had to do was to argue about them, they were things which changed completely according to what one said about them, or the way one looked. Whether they had a

substratum of reality in themselves or not did not concern me, I could leave that to the philosophers to argue
about, but what appeared to me was a never-ending
murmuring sea of space all about me, above my head,
beneath my feet and on every side. Whatever happened,
while awake I could never escape it. All I could do was
to some extent make deliberate choice of the part of the
sea I would look at and under my looking it at once took
shape. I open my eyes (I had shut them in the effort to
express this clearly) and find myself looking at my desk,
aware of it heavy and solid, in my room, on the top floor
looking out over the garden, in a familiar street, in
London. . . . I can go on a long time, making a more and
more complicated net-work which spreads its form out
on all sides and shapes the enveloping vagueness, like the
thin patterning of ice which begins to film across a pond
in the stillness of winter woods at nightfall, fixing the
idly floating leaves immovable. If I shut my eyes now so
that I cannot see my desk, the chirp of sparrows becomes
the centre of my thought, now making its pattern against
the murmuring dark emptiness of space. Again if I choose
I can send out the streamers of my thought on every side,
fixing the sound in the knowledge of the roof above my
window, the sky above that, the garden beneath, London
all around set in England in the spring full of chirping
birds, and beyond that . . . and on further as before. If I
put my fingers in my ears, then a buzzing in them stands
out against the remoter buzzing of space. Whatever I do
there is always some central core of my thought standing
out in a clear pattern against an all-enveloping vagueness. The central core stretching out into vagueness may
be in any terms; it may be concerned with external
things, what is happening around me, or else with what
is going on in my own head, remembered or imagined

scenes, a tune, voices, or a silent talking to myself: 'I wish I was in the garden.... How on earth am I going to get this finished before five o'clock!' But this core does not have clear-cut edges, it is not like the pattern of a carpet, stopping off short with a border. At any moment there exist in the fringes of my thought faint patternings which can be brought to distinctness when I look at them. Like a policeman with a flash-light I can throw the bright circle of my awareness where I choose; if any shadow or movement in the dim outer circle of its rays arouses my suspicion, I can make it come into the circle of brightness and show itself for what it is. But the beam of my attention is not of fixed width, I can widen or narrow its focus as I choose. To explore the sky for aircraft a searchlight must travel backwards and forwards, sweeping the sky like a broom. My thought can do that, but it has another movement as well; it can widen its beam and survey the whole sky at the same moment, and this widening is something which I can control at will.

When I considered my observations in the light of this idea of wide and narrow attention, it occurred to me that there must be two quite different ways of perceiving. Only a tiny act of will was necessary in order to pass from one to the other, yet this act seemed sufficient to change the face of the world, to make boredom and weariness blossom into immeasurable contentment.

· (1) Narrow attention. – This first way of perceiving seemed to be the automatic one, the kind of attention which my mind gave to everyday affairs when it was left to itself. The psychology books seemed to agree in this. They said that you attend automatically to whatever interests you, whatever seems likely to serve your personal desires; but I could not find anywhere mentioned what seemed to me the most important fact about it, that this kind of attention has a narrow focus, by this means it selects what serves its immediate interests and ignores the rest. As far as I could see it was a 'questing beast', keeping its nose close down to the trail, running this way and that upon the scent, but blind to the wider surroundings. It saw items according to whether they served its purposes, saw them as a means to its own ends, not interested in them at all for their own sake. This attitude was probably essential for practical life, so I supposed that from the biological point of view it had to be one which came naturally to the mind. But since it saw everything in relation to something else, as a means to some end, contentment was always in the future.

(2) Wide attention. – The second way of perceiving seemed to occur when the questing purposes were held in leash. Then, since one wanted nothing, there was no need to select one item to look at rather than another, so it became possible to look at the whole at once. To attend to something and yet want nothing from it, these seemed to be the essentials of the second way of perceiving. I thought that in the ordinary way when we want nothing from any object or situation we ignore it. Or if we are forced to attend to something which does not offer us any means of furthering our desires, then sheer habit makes us attend in the narrow focus way, looking at separate details and being bored. But if by chance we should have discovered the knack of holding wide our attention, then the magic thing happens. This at least was how I explained what had happened to me.

Certainly the transition from narrow to wide attention could sometimes, I thought, be produced voluntarily; but sometimes it seemed to depend also on external conditions or a casual phrase. There were all the times, before I understood at all what I was at, when I had chanced upon it, when sometimes tiredness seemed to lull one's purposes, sometimes mellow weather, sometimes alcohol. Then I would perhaps suddenly find myself breathing deeply in the calm impersonality of shapes or colours, or even in a sudden glimpse of someone's character seen from a view-point that had stepped clear of the distortions of my personal interests. And once when I was lying, weary and bored with myself, on a cliff looking over the Mediterranean, I had said, 'I want nothing', and immediately the landscape dropped its picture-postcard garishness and shone with a gleam from the first day of creation, even the dusty weeds by the roadside. Then again, once when ill in bed, so fretting with unfulfilled purposes that I could not at all enjoy the luxury of enforced idleness, I had found myself staring vacantly at a faded cyclamen and had happened to remember to say to myself, 'I want nothing'. Immediately I was so flooded with the crimson of the petals that I thought I had never before known what colour was.

It seemed odd that my mind should respond so quickly to a phrase, to what seemed mere words, spoken casually, when it could be so mulish about carefully willed intentions.

Thinking over all this, it now occurred to me that there were many experiences which had meaning only when they were considered as a whole. I had read, for instance, that the test of a good picture was that all parts should be related to the whole and essential to the whole. This sounded all right, but I did not understand what it meant until one day I remembered to try out my new-found gesture of deliberately holding my attention wide, and apply it to looking at a picture. Resisting the very strong impulse to pass on and see what the next picture was, I simply stood and waited. Staring at the whole canvas, I now did deliberately what I had once before done out of sheer weariness, when looking at a Cézanne painting. Gradually my mind settled down to complete absorption, oblivious to all but the harmonies of shape and colour which once again took on a life of their own and continued to grow out of the paint the longer I looked. Bearing this in mind, I now thought I understood a little the exasperation of those Philistines who think that ecstatic enjoyment of pictures is sheer affectation. For if I had never happened to discover how to make this act of wide focus so that I could see the whole all at the same time, it would certainly have been affectation to stand for ten minutes in front of one picture and pretend I was not bored.

In spite of all this, however, it was years before I really got it into my head what this second kind of attention really was like; certainly it was utterly different from that vaguely preoccupied dreaming in which I had previously spent all the hours when no active demands were being made upon my thoughts by the outside world. And still I could not always attain it, even when I knew it was necessary. Sometimes the very desire to achieve the pleasures of a wide focus seemed to prevent it happening. Sometimes it seemed as if it was my preconceived idea of what I wanted that was the stumbling-block. This happened particularly whenever there was an 'occasion', something I had looked forward to and felt to be a unique moment of life. Fearful of missing any aspect through inattention, I would often attend so carefully that I missed the whole thing. Then, there being no meaning for me in what was happening, boredom would drive my thoughts to find their own interests and wander off into those private preoccupations from which I was always trying to escape. So, in the midst of watching a play I had longed to see, or talking to a person I had longed to meet, I would be outraged to discover that I had missed unrecoverable moments in idle reverie about a new dress, and what So-and-so would say when they saw it. I am reminded of once attending an ice-hockey match. I had begun to watch with my usual attitude, 'Here's something to be attended to', narrowly focusing my mind upon individual players, but from the very outset I was chagrined to find myself wasting this long-looked-forward-to occasion in preoccupations about my personal affairs. Then I remembered to widen my awareness and was at once entranced with delight at the ever-changing total picture of the game, and at my ability to see the character, not only the items, of each man's movement.

Now also it gradually occurred to me that expectancy might be an obstruction to one's power of seeing which was particularly active in the sphere of emotion. It seemed inevitable that from romantic stories, plays, films, one should be always picking up, unknowingly, standards of what should be the ideal relationship between two people. I know I had once or twice found myself turning away discontented from what I had, because it was not what the romances had taught me to expect. Of course as soon as I really looked at the standard I was judging by I saw its absurdity and knew at once that real life was not like that; but it was a long time before I had realized that any standard was there. When at last I did recognize this obstruction to my view, then I was able, at least sometimes, to sweep all ideas away from my mind so that immediately real experience, new and indescribable, flooded in.

But if expectancy of delight was a stumbling-block, so that vivid pictures of what might happen shut me off from perceiving what actually did happen, an even greater impediment was expectancy of failure. For here the ingrained habit of a lifetime seemed invariably towards contraction. As soon as the fear of making a mistake rose in my mind, then the act of wide attention became almost impossible. For the more I realized the difficulty, the more I tried and focused my attention to a pin-point, like an internal screwing-up of one's eyes to see better.

*

So it was that I came to the conclusion that the ordinary everyday perception of things which serves us pretty well when going about daily practical affairs is not the only kind of perceiving that the mind can do. It seemed certain that there was another kind also, which produced quite different results and was far more detached and disinterested. The first kind seemed to be deeply ingrained in my habits of thinking, and it was only on occasions, sometimes voluntarily, sometimes by inadvertence, that I could emerge into the second kind. But whenever I did, it brought a quality of delight completely unknown to the first kind. The voluntary gestures which I had previously observed as leading to moments of great contentment seemed then to have been simply ways in which I had stumbled upon this kind of perception. They were all ways in which I deliberately restrained that continual effort after purposes which seemed the natural condition of everyday perceiving. So also were my formal exercises in concentration; by fixing my thought upon a single object I automatically restrained it from purposes and forced disinterestedness upon it. My next task was to find out why I could not see things in this way more often.

CHAPTER VIII

Discovering that Thought can be Blind

> I went to work upon this boat the most like a fool that ever
> man did who had any of his senses awake. I pleased myself
> with the design without determining whether I was ever
> able to undertake it; not but that the difficulty of launching
> my boat came often into my head; but I put a stop to my
> own inquiries into it by this foolish answer which I gave
> myself – 'Let me first make it, I'll warrant that I'll find some
> way or other to get it along when it is done'.
>
> This was a most preposterous method; but the eagerness
> of my fancy prevailed, and to work I went and felled a
> cedar-tree.
>
> DANIEL DEFOE

I HAD now discovered certain facts about the way my
mind behaved. I had come to the conclusion that what
mattered most to me seemed to depend on my powers of
perceiving, and that these were, to some extent, under
my own control. But the greatest obstacle in the way
which was continually preventing me from being fully
responsive to my surroundings seemed to be fear of difficulty. I thought then that my next task must be to look
for reasons why I was always expecting things to be difficult, distrusting my own ability, fearing the criticisms of
others.

At first I did not find any more help in scientific explanations than I had done before. I had of course heard
a lot of talk which purported to explain such attitudes in
terms of current psychological doctrine – 'unconscious
guilt feelings', 'inferiority complex', and the like. But
though I understood that it was all supposed to be due
to situations of my early childhood, I did not see how to
apply such explanations to the particular problem which

I had in hand. So I had floundered on, still blindly, until several years after I had begun to keep a diary – until, in fact, I was introduced to some experimental studies which eventually shed a flood of light on all my observations, although it took me many years to grasp their full implications.

The experiments dealt with the question of how children think. As far as I could understand it, the central discovery seemed to be that a most crucial step in the mental development of a child is learning how to distinguish between thoughts and things. It appeared that, at first, mental happenings must be indistinguishable from physical ones, for a child is not born knowing that what goes on in his own mind has not the same sort of independent existence as what goes on around him. He does not know that a feeling in his own mind is only his feeling, he has no means of telling, for instance, that the whole world is not darkened with his misery; for he cannot know, until he has laboriously experimented, which of the things he is aware of is part of himself, which is independent. Neither does he know that his feeling, a momentary boredom or pang of hunger, will not go on for ever like a table or a chair, for he has not yet learnt that feelings and ideas are things which pass. It follows that any discomfort is utterly overwhelming, for he cannot see it against the background of his past experience, and look forward knowing that it will soon be over. When his mother leaves him she has gone for ever, the misery of loneliness is 'all there is'.*

His view of the world follows as a direct result of this ignorance that thought is different from things. For him things *are* what they *seem* to be, so that he believes that

*J. Piaget, *Language and Thought of the Child* (and other later works) (Kegan Paul, 1926); S. Isaacs, *The Nursery Years* (Routledge, 1929).

the sun does in fact accompany his walks because it appears to. And words are like thoughts, they too have the same sort of reality as tables and chairs, so that to think about an act or to speak of it is as good as doing it, and if he repeats a statement often enough, or wishes for something hard enough, he can make it happen. For he does not know that an idea is something private and provisional, which needs to be tested before you can be sure that it corresponds to facts in the external world. To him an imagined dragon is as terrifying as a real one, for he does not know what 'only imagination' means. So also he has at first no knowledge of error, no knowledge that an idea may be mistaken, because for him, if something can be thought or said, then it is true, and there is no need to withhold judgement until the statement is proved. For the same reason he believes all sorts of fantastic ideas about the causes of natural events, or the results of his actions, such as what will happen if he is naughty, ideas that are not borne out at all by his everyday experience. And he also believes contradictory ideas, for he sees no need to look for consistency between one statement and another. It follows also that he is self-centred, not because he has an unpleasant nature, but because he is as yet ignorant of the very existence of any other mind than his own, since he knows his own, not *as* a mind, but as the 'all' of his experience.

I gathered then that the psychologists made a very important distinction between the kind of childish thinking which results from the fact that thought is not aware of its own private and personal nature, and the common-sense reasoning which recognizes the existence of an external world independent of ideas and wishes. The transition from one kind of thinking to the other seemed to occur as a result of opposition. A child gradually discovers both that the physical world opposes his desires, that it cannot be wheedled into obeying him, and also that what is in his mind is not necessarily in other people's, so that in order to make other people do what he wants he must express his thoughts in words and produce reasons for his demands. By this means he is gradually led to look at his own thought and see it for what it is.

Although these experiments dealt only with children, I felt certain that they had a very important bearing upon my own problems. But since the main characteristic of the first kind of thought was that it was unconscious, it followed that if by any chance one had failed to grow out of it completely one would still not be directly aware of the fact. This suggested that it might be interesting to try to explore further the part of my thought of which I was not generally aware and find out how it behaved.

I decided that I would begin by a study of my wandering thought. I knew that I was much given to daydreaming, that my mind was always slipping away to irrelevant subjects when it should have been upon my work, that I was often preoccupied when people were talking and did not listen properly to what they said. I knew also that I felt vaguely guilty about this, and was afraid that it was a habit which would eventually catch me out in some critical situation. I was always falling back exhausted from the effort to concentrate, slipping into that state of blind submergence in which I passively followed my nosing thought in its wanderings. This seemed to be a state of peculiar blindness, for although I had the feeling that I could have said at any moment more or less what I was thinking if I had been asked, yet I did not ask it of myself, so did not in fact know. And when I did begin to try and find where my wandering attention had been to, I found it none too easy, for this free-drifting thought was a shy creature. If I did try to watch it too obviously it would scuttle away into its hole only to appear again as soon as I turned my head the other way. Finally I found that it was only by observing out of the corner of my eye and then immediately trying to fix what I had seen in words, that I could gain any clear idea of what was there. Even then I felt that the effort to put the idea into words somehow distorted its shape.

After a little practice I learnt how to trace a train of thought back from any particular moment. I would suddenly say to myself, 'What am I thinking about?' and then, 'What was the thought that came before it, and the one before that ... ?' and so on. I could never follow these trains of ideas back very far but I could go far enough to give myself a general idea of their nature. Here is one of the first of such attempts, a train of ideas observed when I was not particularly worried about anything, the moment being chosen simply in order to get an idea of the subject matter of my casual everyday preoccupations:

Oughtn't we to ask those people in to tea? That's best, say, 'Do you ever have time for a cup of tea? Will you come in any day?' Say we are free all the week, let them choose, will the maid answer the door? will she be too busy? what shall we give them? go into town and buy a cake? will they expect it? can't afford these extras, but bread and jam won't do, what does one give people for tea ... why not something a little unusual? cress sandwiches? but it's too late for cress, tomato and brown bread? p'raps they've not had that before, but tomatoes are a shilling a pound. ... I must introduce P., I mustn't forget, will she like them – what's that noise? horses galloping in the field, there they are, how the sound carries, lovely things, it sounds as if the ground were dry but isn't, what must a cavalry charge sound like then? – that young man in the village, he stood aside most discreetly while I climbed the ladder, his brown arm with

the wrist strap, how nice they were, what was in his mind?
will they tell stories and laugh over it, the old men in the
village? . . .

There was certainly nothing very arresting about this,
but it served to show me that this method of tracing back
my unwitting thoughts was at least possible, and later I
was able to apply it in situations when to know my own
hidden attitudes was a most urgent matter.

Another trick that I discovered was to keep myself
particularly alert to any little movements going on in
the back of my mind, passing ideas which were often
quite irrelevant to my task of the moment and which I
would never have noticed in the ordinary way. I called
these 'butterflies', for they silently fluttered in from no-
where and were gone in a moment. A typical instance
was when, in the middle of an emotional crisis, a 'scene'
with someone, I would be aware of a little far-away voice
hinting at the back of my mind that my tears were not
quite uncontrollable, that I was really staging the emotion in order to prove something to myself – or perhaps
in order to get something from the other person. Once or
twice even I was able to turn round upon myself quickly
enough to catch the real intention and fix it in words. For
instance:

I *must* make a scene, *must* be miserable, when he says that,
I'll cry, I mustn't let him know it's better, I won't say I'm
happy, for he won't help me any more, he'll leave me to
manage alone.

By means of such devices I was eventually able to gain
a fair idea of how my thought behaved when left to itself.
One of the first things that struck me was its inconse-
quence and irresponsibility. I noticed that if I could not
at once see how I was going to fit a certain action in with
my other plans I immediately thought about something

quite different. I could never predict what would be in my mind the next moment, and I was often amazed at the way these thoughts completely ignored what I felt to be important occasions. They seemed at times like the swarm of tiny beetles which skate on the surface of a pond, never diving to any real issue – an airy skimming in endless mazes.

One of my next observations was that I seemed very liable to assume that because something was said it must therefore be true. I would listen to one person's story of a quarrel and believe it as absolute fact, never remembering that thought is relative, that I was listening only to one view of the situation and that when I met the partner to the quarrel I would hear quite a different version. I would read a book review, accepting the judgement given as the final truth, and then, when I happened on a second review of the same book giving a different opinion, I would feel quite lost and confused. The same thing happened when I read the newspapers. I would believe implicitly whatever I read in any paper about political affairs, finding it almost impossible to remember to withhold my acceptance of what was said until I had also heard other opinions.

All this certainly seemed very like the child's mistake which I had read about, the tendency to assume that whatever idea was in my mind at the moment must be real, must be fact in the same sense that tables and chairs are facts. Even when two opposing opinions were presented to me simultaneously I did not learn to judge between them, I merely felt lost, confusedly swaying from one to the other, quite unable to realize each as a partial and individual view, each contributing something from which I might draw in order to create a third opinion. It also occurred to me now that this might explain why I was so desperately dependent upon what people thought of me. For to childish thinking, the fact that something had been said made it true.

Then I began to observe that not only opinions but moods also had an absolute quality. Sometimes I found that in my happy moments I could not believe that I had ever been miserable, I planned for the future as if happiness were all there was; while in my moments of despair I could not even remember what happiness felt like, and the whole future was black.

I found also that this kind of thinking did really believe in its own power to alter fact. Several times when I had made some stupid mistake I caught my mind going over the incident again and again, as if by thinking hard enough what I ought to have done I could undo the mistake and make it as though it had not happened.

I then began to catch 'butterflies' which showed me quite clearly that this kind of thinking also takes it for granted that oneself is something absolute and special, as if it could never really remember to take into account the existence of other minds. When troubles came to me I heard part of myself saying incredulously: 'That this should have happened to ME! To think that *I* should have to find my life not as I would have chosen!' although I knew perfectly well that things of the same sort happen to everyone. And certainly my thought was quite oblivious of the private character of its ideas. It mistook them for things of such absolute importance that it was often filled with incredulous indignation when other people did not adapt themselves to suit it. Just as a child says, 'Naughty table!' when it bumps its head, and thinks the wind is blowing 'on purpose', so when my affairs were going badly I was constantly catching butterflies of resentment, attempts to make out that it was all So-and-so's *fault.* I found myself planning telling phrases in which I would make known to them just what I thought of them, fully convinced that if they only knew what I thought of them they would surely feel ashamed of themselves and at once put things right.

She's a slacker, a slacker, if only she knows she'll change, she must, I'll tell her, I'll say 'You're such an awful slacker' ... I'll goad her into seeing it so she'll stop being one, she must.

It never occurred to such thinking that people might not be making difficulties deliberately, that they were not completely in control of their own actions. Why the idea of unwitting action was beyond the range of my blind thinking puzzled me. But the fact that it was so was abundantly clear, not only from my own butterfly-catching, but from frequent observations of, for instance, harassed parents trying to deal with a difficult child. I had seen well-educated and cultured mothers apparently quite unable to recognize, during their moments of exasperation, that a child's nervous habits, bed-wetting, stammering, or what not, might be quite beyond the child's direct control and were certainly not done 'only to annoy'. I myself found this tendency to believe in the wilfulness of others so strong, when under emotional stress, that I even found myself planning punishments, or sometimes dramatic demonstrations of the state of misery their actions had reduced me to. Here is such a butterfly caught in a moment of acute emotion, remembered and written down later:

He won't do what I want, he doesn't care ... but I'll show him, he'll have to in the end. ... I could refuse to go and see him – that's no good, he wouldn't mind – I could run away somewhere, go wild about the streets, run amok, hurt myself, *make* him take notice, *make* him feel sorry, feel sorry how he's hurt me, make him help me, be nice to me. ... I'll kill myself to punish him, so he'll have to be sorry. . . . That's no good, he'll guess, he'll see through it, shrug his shoulders, say, 'If she wants to hurt herself . . .'

Here was I contemplating killing myself to make someone do as I wished, and sucking comfort from the thought of the offender's remorse, quite oblivious of the fact that I would not be there to see it. Actually this particular train of thought continued, and in the later part showed a tendency to emerge from such complete irrationality, perhaps because I was observing it with half an eye, even through my tears; for the next sentence reads:

. . . that won't do, for I shall know that I'm doing it on purpose . . . what *can* I do then to escape this thing in me that knows I'm doing it on purpose, that tells me I'll have to behave sensibly in the end? . . . go mad, *then* I should not know . . . then I could do things to make them care and there would be nothing to hold me back.

I suspect it was the thought expressed in this final sentence which actually brought me to myself again and shocked me into awareness of what I had been thinking in time to go over it and record the main part. I remember 'coming-to' with a flash of understanding which dissipated all my impotent rage in a moment, for I was delighted at having caught myself out in such a flagrant piece of absurdity and pinned down such a super-butterfly.

This was not an isolated instance, although the most dramatic. I find a butterfly noted in my diary at a time when my affairs were not progressing as I wished, 'I want to give a lot of people a lot of trouble'. So I began to feel I understood those children who figure in the police courts for having vented their outraged feelings in some scandalous escapade, in truancy and stealing. I began to realize what a lot there was to be learnt about the unrecognized parts of oneself from observation of unhappy children. For instance, I once found myself making a quite unnecessary fuss over some difficulty, and managed to catch the idea that if I showed enough distress some-one would come and help me. Actually the problem was, like most of the difficulties of adult life, one which no one else could solve for me, so this observation gave me a clue as to a possible cause of many of my ineptitudes and confessions of failure. As a child, if I cried and said, 'This is too difficult, I can't do it', someone came and helped me. Now I found myself one day unwilling to admit I was happy because of a vague sense that I might thereby forgo some advantage, might give up my claim to that special attention which seemed to be the prerogative of the miserable.

CHAPTER IX

Watching the Antics of Blind Thinking

I observe myself and so I come to know others.

JUST as I had discovered earlier that when I let my thoughts write themselves they had quite unexpected things to say, so I was now finding that whenever I managed to turn round upon my thought and catch it red-handed I was not at all sure of finding that amount of common sense which I had fondly supposed myself to possess. With this in mind I set out therefore to find what further effects of this blind thinking might be shown in my daily behaviour.

My first observations were concerned with anger and bad temper. For instance, I would sometimes find myself raging against someone whose behaviour had interfered with my wishes, feel a longing to impose my will upon them, and then, the more they failed to do as I wanted, the more was I impelled to act as I would in the world of things, by physical force. My thought would even be reduced to such a primitive level that throwing things at the offender appeared to be the only way of making him do what I wanted; as, in a modern play that I had seen, the wife broke a gramophone record over her husband's head in order to make him agree with her. I realized then that a kind of thinking which could not recognize thought for what it is could certainly not be aware of the complexity of motives which might prompt another person's act. Even though I had learned long ago that it was 'not done' to try to control others by throwing things at them, my blind thought still wanted to rush into action. Sometimes, however, when my mind became obsessed with such an impulse, sheer exhaustion from the ideas going round and round in my head would drive me to remember my act of detachment. I would be forced to stand back from my thought, and to refrain from constant planning, so I was able to ask, not 'How can I make them do what I want?' but 'Why are they behaving like this?' The sense of relief and freedom which always followed when I managed to bring myself to ask, 'What are the facts?' instead of, 'What shall I do?' was like waking up from one of those tiresome dreams in which one is continually involved in futile efforts, such as trying to pack and catch a train and everything goes wrong.

In general it appeared that my wandering thoughts certainly fitted into the description of childish thinking. It certainly cared very little about the facts at all. Its ideas were guided by feelings, it believed on the whole just what it wanted to believe, though it always liked to pretend that it had taken the facts into account and acted reasonably. Especially did it try to juggle with the facts of time. I would, for example, suddenly get a mood for doing odd household jobs and be so carried away with the feeling of virtue at doing what ought to have been done weeks ago that I would plan and begin half a dozen jobs when there was only time to finish one properly. This tendency really caused me a lot of bother, I always had so many things I wanted to do and this blind thinking would imagine it could do everything. It was always saying in planning the day, 'I'll do this and that, and that, and that . . .' and then would gradually realize that the list was getting too long; but since it could not put one item beside another to compare and decide which was the most urgent I just suffered under an ever-growing burden of too many things to be done. I usually ended by getting a headache and then doing something quite irrelevant which was not on my list of intended jobs at all.

Of course it also meant that my bigger aims were conflicting and confused. For this kind of thought seemed able to take to itself any ideal, however misfitting. Seeing a person it admired it would say, 'I'd like to be like that!' and start fretting to become it, quite ignoring the fact that the ideal chosen might be incompatible with my temperament or the rest of my aims. Like Bottom, it seemed to think it could play every part; like a caddis worm, it seized on every bit of floating rubbish to build into its house. I began to discover that nearly always when I felt overburdened or full of despair it was because I had confused aims, and was trying to do two incompatible things at the same time. Lightly formed intentions mounted up into a hopeless burden of unreached goals so that I went my ways with a heavy sense of failure through always 'meaning to do' something more.

I noticed another thing which also occurred to follow from this disrespectful attitude to facts. It would look for explanations of my difficulties and would plan ways of solving them, but its explanations and its plans were always liable to take a one-sided view of the situation. When I was deliberately trying to think out a problem I would attempt to review all the facts, wait to give my final judgement till I had considered the whole field. But my blind thought seemed incapable of doing this, it seemed in too much of a hurry to get at least some idea which would make it feel comfortable. For instance, I noticed that it was very fond of rehearsing things I was going to say to people. This in itself was of course a very practical habit, for it often gave me a chance to find words beforehand for some meaning which would have been too elusive in the hurry of conversation, leaving me tongue-tied. But although my blind thought went over and over the things I intended to say, it always omitted to imagine what the other person would answer. It just saw them vaguely as a sympathetic and admiring audience, so that when the occasion actually arrived and I did in fact say what I had planned, there was almost inevitably a thud of disappointment. For whatever they responded, whether argument or laughter or silence, it was not what I had expected (although I could easily have foreseen such a response if I had stopped to think), so it put me out of my stride.

Also, since this blind thinking appeared to be incapable of taking an all-round view of any situation, it could never make well-founded decisions. This meant that one could never feel quite sure of anything, for at any moment some accident of thought might throw into the foreground facts which had not been taken into account, which would then oust those upon which the first decision had been based. The result would often be a complete reversal of the decision.

In addition to this inability to see all the facts blind thinking also showed a tendency to distort those facts it did see. I found that its judgements were hardly ever moderate. It liked 'either-or' statements, wanted everything to be all good or all bad. Gradually I became aware how frequently it tried to bolt to extremes. I would find myself assuming perhaps that my work was very good, and then plunging to the opposite attitude as soon as I came up against an inevitable fact showing me that it was not perfect. I would find myself swinging from attitudes of superiority to inferiority and back again with most disconcerting suddenness. Half the time I would feel submissive, only fit to listen respectfully, and the other feel myself a superior intelligence, far above what was going on. Particularly did this tendency to extremes affect my attitude to success. Either I and mine must be altogether to be admired, or else, when I myself could not help seeing more merit in what was someone else's or an obvious flaw in what was mine, then I must be altogether a failure. And in the moment of swinging over I felt a gnawing empty fear, a terrified giving-up and sinking into lifelessness because I was that other thing, a failure, no good. It seemed quite beyond the power of my blind thought to recognize a middle way, to see that most of the things I was concerned about were probably neither the best which ever had been nor yet the worst.

It had another trick. I have already described how it could only be aware of a very limited range of ideas at any one moment and could not combine apparently con-flicting themes. Now I found that it did have a dim no-tion of the ideas which there was not room for it to keep in mind, but that it was inclined to deal with these by imputing them to other people. If I was in an elated mood and what I was doing seemed to me very good in-deed, then the banished self-criticism would appear to me as imagined disparaging remarks by other people. If, as often happened, I wanted to do two irreconcilable things, the desire which was not uppermost at the mo-ment would seem to belong to someone else. For instance, at one time it happened that in order to achieve certain things I wanted I had to undertake work that went very much against the grain. When the mood of rebellion against this was dominant I caught myself railing against others as if I were being compelled by them to do this thing that I hated, quite slurring over the fact that it was my own ambitions which were driving me to it. It was as if my excluded thoughts, if I refused to give them expression, would find it for themselves, like bubbles which must eventually reach the surface. And they would find expression by silently biasing my view of the world around me. Sometimes my hatred of some part of myself which I would not accept became a hatred of someone else, and I would say all sorts of things about that person, but anyone who was perceiving could tell that I was really speaking about myself. If only I could remember and know that half the things which people said about the world did tell me useful facts, particularly when spoken with vehemence, but did not tell what the speakers intended. For they were not giving me facts about the world, but facts about themselves.

Just as blind thinking had no sense of time in planning things, so it seemed unable to distinguish between the past and the present. Since any idea which occurred to it was absolute for the moment, a chance memory from the remote past would seem just as real and important as what was happening now. So I would sometimes catch myself out in a burst of rage about nothing, or tongue-tied with nervousness of people from whom I had nothing to fear; and then realize that this emotion did not fit the present situation at all, it was only that my blind thought had been reminded of the past by some chance likeness, and had then behaved as if the present were the past. For example, I once found myself struggling desperately to assert my independence when there was actually no one threatening it, just because, without knowing it, I had been accidentally reminded of the days when I was the youngest and most dependent person in my family. Apparently it was only 'seeing' thought which could say, 'That's all over and done with', blind thought was at the mercy of blind habit and accidental resemblances.

It seemed that this curious confusion of past and present was possible because blind thinking completely ignored the laws of logic. For it, a thing could be both itself and something else at the same time. I would be quite aware in my own mind that some person I was afraid of was of course not my father, and yet I would continually behave towards him as if he were – just as in dreams a figure can seem to be two people at once. Endless self-deceptions were of course possible for thinking of this kind. I would do something both for creditable reasons and mean personal ones, and yet my logical mind, not realizing the possibility of such confusion, would quite honestly see the one set of motives only.

As I gradually became more and more familiar with the ways of this blind thinking I came to the conclusion that the success of my whole enterprise hung on my ability to emerge from it. For I realized that it made learning by experiment quite impossible. The essence of experiment is to have some desire or plan and then to try various methods of bringing about what one wants, always keeping in mind the first intention and comparing what actually happened with what was expected to happen. My blind thought, however, having set out full of intentions, would, with the first unexpected incident, become distracted and set off in another direction, like a child who goes to fetch something but forgets its plan because it finds something more interesting to do on the way. Apparently it could not hold the unexpected happening in mind side by side with the intention and so revise its method in order to fit the new facts. So it was that I had set out boldly saying, 'I will experiment with life and so make for myself rules about how to live', and I had plunged into experiences only to find when I came out that I could conclude nothing from them, and could find no rule for future guidance, because I could not put my knowledge of the experience side by side with my intention and see where I had been wrong. All I could do was to drift blindly from one experience to another, vaguely hoping that if enough things happened to me I would eventually learn wisdom. I never realized that I was making the same mistake again and again, simply because I did not know how to emerge from blind thinking into that state of seeing in which reflexion and the drawing of conclusions were possible.

There was another result of this inability to see more than one thing at once. Since it could not compare experiences, my blind thought could have no sense of values. Like a child telling a story it was quite vague about prepositions, it liked to link all its ideas together with 'and then'. For instance, I would plan with my husband that we would buy something we wanted *if* we managed to save on something else, but my blind thinking would forget the 'if' and I would find that I was buying what we wanted in any case, quite oblivious of the condition upon which the plan had depended. So also the trivial and the important could share an equal sense of urgency, since always the concern of the moment was the most important whatever it was. This meant that any trifling worry might spread its cloud over the whole landscape and I was therefore liable to busy myself with a momentary detail when vital issues were hanging in the balance. Now I saw how it was that I could make up lists of things I liked, or of what made me happy, writing each item that came into my head, but could not decide which was the most important. I saw also how it was that when I had let my thoughts write themselves there had emerged such a swarm of apparently unconnected and irrelevant ideas from the depths of my past experience.

At this stage I tried to make some sort of summary of the habits and results of this kind of thinking which so often formed a chattering accompaniment at the back of my mind to all I did. In the first place, then, this chattering mind was an unreasonable mind, it was liable to cling to its own view of the facts quite regardless of distortions and contradictions. It was also a mean mind, it seemed unable to escape from the narrow circle of its own interests, it recognized only itself and was always trying to force the rest of the world to do the same. Further, in the face of the hard facts of my own imperfections it set me all sorts of impossible standards without my knowing it. It wanted me to be the best, cleverest, most beautiful creature, and made me feel that if I was not all of these things then I was the extreme opposite, the dregs of creation and utterly lost. And it did not tell me that it was doing this, for if it had I should have seen at once how absurd it was. It only went on spinning its web of glowing pictures, pictures of myself doing and being heroic things, quietly chattering the admiration with which my achievements were to be acclaimed. And I, poor fool, had been led into taking this for a real and reasonable goal, so that everything which subsequently fell short of it was vaguely disappointing.

Such, then, were the antics of my undirected thought. Apparently, behind all my carefully judged common-sense attitudes to life, there was this undercurrent of a totally different kind of thinking. In the ordinary way I should never have suspected its existence, but since I had now discovered it I could not doubt that it was capable of influencing my feelings and actions to a very great extent. For every act that I did which was based on deliberate choice in accordance with a standard I had preferred, there must be dozens which grew out of this inconsequent, irrational, self-centred and self-distorted reverie; for I knew that the moments when I was really aware of my thought were not very frequent.

Having discovered the tremendous power of this blind thinking to distort my purposes and play havoc with my peace, I came more and more to understand the intricacies of behaviour in others as well as in myself; and eventually also this study did lead me to understand the causes of those continually present fears which had so often prevented me from emerging into the fresh air of wide, purposeless attention.

CHAPTER X

The Escape from Blind Thinking

A man must see and study his vice to correct it; they who
conceal it from others, commonly conceal it from themselves; and do not think it close enough, if they themselves
see it: they withdraw and disguise it from their own con-
sciences: *Quare vitia sua nemo confitetur? Quia etiam nunc illis est;
somnium narrare, vigilantis est.* (Why does no man confess his
vices? Because he is yet in them; 'tis for a waking man to
tell his dream.) The diseases of the body explain themselves
by their increase; we find that to be the gout, which we call
a rheum or a strain; the diseases of the soul, the greater they
are, keep themselves the most obscure; the most sick are the
least sensible.

MONTAIGNE

HAVING once made the guess that I had not entirely
grown out of this childhood tendency to confuse thought
with things, I began to ask what such development might
depend on. Apparently that part of thinking which is
concerned with knowing the external physical world soon
emerges as a result of what we are expressly taught. I no
longer think the moon accompanies me when I go for a
walk, for although it still seems as if it did, I have acquired the special knowledge which convinces me that it
is not so. But the part of my thinking which is concerned
with knowledge of my own and other people's minds
does not seem to have received such effective attention in
my education. I wondered why it was easy for me to
learn that what appears to me at the moment in the
world of things is not all there is, but in the world of
emotion and thought it is so difficult to learn this. I may
have been told only once that the moon has its own orbit
and does not care whether I go for a walk or not: yet I

believe it. But although it must have been impressed upon me time and again during my early years that other people have their rights, their own desires that are separate from mine, and that my thoughts and impulses are not all there is, I never seem able to hold the knowledge permanently. Often, when impatiently waiting for a bus that does not come, I catch myself falling into a burst of rage against the driver, feeling as if his action could only refer to me, and he were deliberately dawdling because he knew I was in a hurry.

My first clue to this problem was the observation that these antics of childish thought occurred particularly when I was under the influence of emotion. It was only when the lateness of the bus made it seem likely that I would miss an appointment that I began to think the driver was doing it on purpose. It was only when I was running to catch a train that I became convinced people were getting in my way deliberately. This observation gave me the idea that emotion did something to one's thinking, pulled it down from its ordinary level of understanding. It was as if there must be a certain degree of heat to fuse the little lumps of past knowledge and present experience into one whole. It seemed to me that emotion, perhaps by taking energy to itself, lowered the temperature of my thinking below the melting point of its different metals so that the lump of the moment's thought remained isolated, filling my mind to the exclusion of all else. In this state I could not remember my slowly acquired knowledge that other people have independent feelings and lives of their own, I could not see beyond the magic circle of my own rage, so everything that others did referred to me alone. I also noticed that the same sort of thing happened when I was tired, for then worries which I knew were really unimportant would often come to dominate my mind completely. I had long ago learnt that what at night appeared to be an irretrievable disaster would probably shrink to a quite trivial mishap by the time I woke up in the morning. I had noticed too that illness had the same effect, it lowered my capacity for seeing things in proportion almost to a minimum; in fact, all kinds of bodily conditions appeared to influence the maturity of thought and the capacity for perceiving. I had also observed what a complete reversal of mood was brought about, for instance, by a meal; if I was tired and miserable, then eating improved matters, but if I was ecstatically happy, then a meal always broke the spell. Clearly, then, physical conditions played a very important part in determining the quality of my thought: but I did not think this was the whole story, and anyhow I could not always avoid being tired. I therefore tried to approach the problem from the opposite angle.

If emotion and fatigue lowered the potency of thought, what raised it? I began to reconsider my moments of delight in terms of this statement of the problem, moments whose essential quality had been a fusing of experience, a flash of significance uniting the meaningless and separate. If one assumed that thinking was a process involving some form of energy, it seemed quite appropriate to imagine my gesture of holding back from mental action as causing an accumulation of energy which automatically raised the potency. By preventing energy from continually flowing away in a noisy stream of efforts and purposes I could make it fill up into a silent pool of clearness.

But this gesture of restraining mental effort which brought me such delight had been concerned almost entirely with perception of external things. When, however, I was concerned only with inner cogitations the problem appeared to be somewhat different, for then what passed before me was so ethereal as to be almost invisible unless I gave it form. I could not stand back and look at it, because I hardly knew it was there.

When considering this, I remembered reading that it was a great day in a child's mental development when he learnt to tell a deliberate lie, for this meant the implicit understanding that thought was different from things and could be dealt with separately. This made me consider how it was that I had ever come to realize that thought existed independently; I saw that words, pictures and all symbols helped me to realize it because in giving thought concrete form they made it into something which could be argued about, tested, compared. When, however, it had no such concrete form I was so submerged in it that my thought could not see itself, with the result that I could not deliberately control it at all. Now I saw too a possible reason why sometimes a single verbal expression of preoccupations had seemed to act like a magic incantation upon my mood. It had perhaps just served to externalize my thought so that I could stand apart and look at it.

Now also I could see that once an idea was stated it was exposed to the light of common sense, and whatever absurdities of childish thinking it might contain would not remain long unchallenged, if not by myself, then sooner or later by others. I supposed, then, that the reason why many of my wandering thoughts still contained childish distortions, even when I was not carried away by emotion, was that they dealt with subjects that I had never really tried to put into words.

Bearing this in mind, I now tried to compare my way of dealing with ideas that interested me, ideas which I had accepted as legitimate subjects for thought, with those which I had repudiated as too painful or too shameful to be considered. I saw that whenever I caught my drifting thought busy with a subject of the first kind I was eager to carry it further and to reach conclusions, to formulate my opinion in words so that I might tell someone about it or else express it in action. If the idea first occurred, as it usually did, in a vague formless state, a half-glimpsed vista of possibilities, I would seize upon it, force it into words, and it would persist in my mind till I felt that I had formulated as much of the idea as I could. But if there were signs that my thought was approaching a subject of the second kind, one which I did not like to think of, I immediately, without knowing what I did, turned my thoughts in a different direction, leaving the subject I had shied at in its original formlessness.

I now asked myself what might be happening when my thought was neither completely passive, as in daydreaming, nor completely self-directed, as in thinking out a logical problem. What was it doing when it responded half-automatically to the demands of whatever situation I happened to be in; for example, during conversations? Here my thoughts could not run their course uninterrupted, as they did when I was sewing or gardening, for conversation demanded something more than complete passivity, it required at least a minimum of choice and judgement, and because of this the quality of thought was different. The demands of social life acted as though someone were continually asking me, 'What are you thinking about?' And if I were not to be judged a complete bore, I had to be constantly emerging from my private reverie, and giving expression to parts of my mental landscape in terms that would mean something to my companions.

This seemed to do for me automatically what I had found so difficult to do with deliberate intent; that is, it raised my cogitations up from that submerged level in which I could see nothing beyond what appeared to me at the moment. Obviously, I could not indulge in conversation without very soon discovering that my remarks did not find social acceptance as long as they were based on the assumption (even though it were an unwitting assumption) that my own mind was all there was. So because of the instinctive desire not to be shut off from contact with other people, I was forced to realize the private nature of my own thinking, I was forced to stand back from it in order to fashion it into terms which had more than an accidental and private meaning, terms which took into account the common interests of the people I was talking to.

But if my aim in talking was mainly sociable – to get on with other people, to make friends – quite clearly there must be a lot of things which I did not talk about. For my private worries would bore others and my private foibles perhaps shock them. What then would happen to ideas on matters which were never talked of because I should feel too ashamed? I had never asked myself this question before, for I had grown up with a hatred of having my personal affairs discussed. When I listened to the personal talk of others I used sometimes to go hot all over, feeling it utterly impossible that I should ever talk like that about myself. I had thought that private affairs should be dealt with privately. What I had not realized was that usually, if I could not bear to deal with them in public, then they were also too painful to be dealt with in the privacy of my own mind. For, unless I was very clear what I was about, I tried to hide the painful thought just as urgently from my own eyes as from those of others.

I seem to have imagined clear thinking to be a skill one was born with, and that it only needed will-power to bring it into play. I had imagined that I should have thoughts first and then be able to talk about them. Now I began to guess that the order must be reversed, that only by talking could I learn how to think. Once I had really learnt how to think, then, and not till then, could I have the capacity to deal silently with my own most intimate difficulties.

Gradually I began to observe more and more examples of the effects of simply putting an unadmitted thought into words, even to myself. One day, for instance, I was trying to make use of one of the internal gestures to bring escape from boredom but not one of them seemed to have any effect. It was a summer day in Cornwall, and yet for me it might as well have been a November fog, for I could take no delight in the sea and cliffs and in being alone on sweet-smelling grass. After much fretting I lay down in exasperation on the edge of the cliff and began trying to put into words anything that might be worrying me. At once I found that I was concerned with a man I had met some days before with whom I had felt a strong and unexpected sympathy, but he had gone his way and I mine without any verbal understanding between us. I had apparently been going over and over the incidents of our meeting, as if half expecting each time to find something more and quite unable to let the matter rest. But I now discovered that with the deliberate speaking of my thoughts to myself, in words, they lost their obsessive quality and also my boredom had entirely disappeared. This rather surprised me, because I thought I had known what I was thinking about all the time, I thought that I could have said at any moment what was bothering me; but apparently the fact that I did not, although I could, made all the difference. It seemed that although dimly aware of what I was thinking, I had been repudiating it and trying to drive the subject from my thoughts by will, partly because I was ashamed of it, partly because I did not want to be distracted from enjoying the summer day. It had therefore remained on the level of that blind thinking which believed in its own magic power to alter facts, which believed that by imagining what might have happened it could somehow make the 'might-have-been' true. Hence the irresistible urge to go over the same incident again and again. It was only when I had admitted to myself deliberately in words what I wanted, that I was able to accept the fact that I had not got it.

By now, therefore, I had sufficient experience of the workings of my own mind, backed up by whatever theoretical knowledge I had been able to absorb, to convince me of the necessity of continually admitting to myself in words those thoughts I was ashamed of. But being convinced that it was necessary did not mean that it was easy to do. I did learn very soon how to know the signs that would tell me when I was evading an unadmitted thought – worry, depression, headache, feelings of rush and over-busyness – but it took me much longer to learn ways of finding the thought that was causing the trouble. Part of my mind seemed in fact quite determined that I should not discover what the trouble was. It put up endless excuses and deceits, it would feign all manner of urgencies to distract my attention, like a bird pretending to trail a broken wing in order that intruders may be drawn away from her nest. Chief of these tricks of distraction was the making of most reasonable reasons to explain my own actions or desires, and the making of further reasons to explain why it was not necessary to look for any hidden thought, since the reason I was giving was so obviously adequate.

*

As a result of these observations I made myself two rules:

(i) The cause of any overshadowing burden of worry or resentment is never what it seems to be.

Whenever it hangs over me like a cloud and refuses to disperse, then I must know that it comes from the area of blind thought and the real thing I am worrying about is hidden from me.

(ii) To reason about such feelings, either in oneself or others, is futile.

I now began to understand why it was no good arguing against obsessive fears or worries, for the source of them was beyond the reach both of reason and common sense. They flourished in the No-man's-land of mind where a thing could be both itself and something else at the same time, and the only way to deal with them was to stop all attempts to be reasonable and to give the thoughts free rein. In dealing with other people this meant just listening while they talked out whatever was in their minds, in dealing with myself it usually meant letting my thoughts write themselves.

Even when I had made this rule, however, the resistance against writing my thoughts at these times was still very strong. I would even occasionally have a vague sense of what absurdity was the real cause of my worry, but I would refuse to admit it, saying to myself: 'There can't be anything unreasonable in what I am doing, I know exactly why I am doing it; there's no earthly need to write, to look for a hidden reason, I *know* it's not that, I know exactly what it is' – and always the more certain I felt, the more certainly I was wrong.

My next task was, then, to find out what sort of ideas these were which it was such an urgent matter to keep hidden from myself, and how they came to be there.

CHAPTER XI

Fear of a Dragon

I had no sleep that night. The farther I was from the occasion of my fright, the greater my apprehensions were; which is something contrary to the nature of things, and especially to the usual practice of all creatures in fear. But I was so embarrassed with my own frightful ideas of the thing, that I formed nothing but dismal imaginations to myself, even though I was now a great way off. Sometimes I fancied it must be the devil. . . .

DANIEL DEFOE

I HAVE described how I came to discover that there were two ways of perceiving: one, my everyday way in which I saw only what concerned me, and saw everything with the narrow vision of personal desires; the other, a way which was difficult, which I achieved only in rare moments, but which brought a contentment beyond the range of personal care and anxiety.

I have also described how I found out from some studies of the minds of children that there were two ways of thinking: one the kind we are usually aware of in ourselves, the common-sense way which recognizes that there is a world of fact independent of our wishes; the other, a legacy of our childhood unrecognized in most of us, which is quite unreasonable, and has the most distorted ideas both about itself and about the world.

I now set out to apply this knowledge, and find whether there was anything in the idea of two ways of thinking which would further explain why I could not always control my attention at will, and emerge from narrow-looking into wide-looking whenever I chose. I realized that what often drove me to attempt to repeat the gesture of wide attention was a mood of stress, irritation or emotional unbalance. I would perhaps be all day in that state which, as children, we were told was the result of 'getting out of bed the wrong side', I would be floundering in a morass of self-pity and be exasperated to tears if anyone spoke to me, wildly struggling to regain serenity. Then I would remember my gestures, or the sometimes magic effect of saying in words what was in my mind. Perhaps in some lovely place, out of doors, among fields, I would find myself quite unresponsive to my surroundings, as if a dense fog enveloped me, and I would try to push myself out of myself, or say: 'There's a pattern of bare branches against a white sky' – charms which had before often freed me into complete self-forgetfulness. But at these times nothing I could do would lift the mood, and I would wait, inert and hopeless, till some chance from outside would break through, often a gentle word from someone, or particularly, I remember, the sight of some gently moving thing – a swan on the Serpentine, clouds sailing overhead, and once, crisp dead leaves on a pond, blown by the wind and scudding like little ships in and out amongst the stagnant oozes.

Brooding over this, there grew in my mind the suspicion that, just as under the influence of emotion my thought was liable to fall back into childish mistakes, so there might also be something in the condition of emotional stress that made my deliberate gestures of attention ineffective. It was as if my mind were some mud-worm which usually, in my everyday perception, burrowed just beneath the surface, but which could on occasion raise its head and emerge into air and daylight. Certainly my internal gesture brought about as startling a change in the face of the world. And perhaps I was not always able to make it because the worm might be burrowing so deep that it could not reach the air just by raising its head. Often it seemed even to forget that it had ever seen the daylight, or the surface of the land, thinking that mud was all there was.

With this picture in mind I began to wonder what might be the nature of those accumulated tensions which made my internal gestures no longer effective. My observations had already given me plenty of hints to show that these tensions were somehow concerned with ideas of difficulty and fear of failure, but now I set out to find whether what I had learned about the ways of blind thinking might not perhaps explain their cause more fully.

Actually I did not begin to understand what I might be afraid of until I had considered some further points about the question of wide and narrow focus of attention. It seemed to me that what the central burning spot of my narrowed attention could do was fuse different parts of experience into the related whole which I call meaning. For instance, I hear a sound in the darkness and it means nothing to me because I hear it with the fringes of my mind, my main attention being busy with the book I am reading. Its meaningless quality startles me, it is ominous; I say 'What was that?' a little breathlessly. It was an isolated sensation and I do not know what to make of it. I cannot go on attending to my book; I wait for the sound to be repeated. When it comes again I am all agog, so that the full beam of my thought flashes upon it and is able to fuse the sensation with knowledge from my past experience, I am now able to give it meaning and say with relief, 'Oh, it's only the cat!' Or what startles me may be, not a sound, not something from outside, but a happening within my mind lurking in the dim fringes beyond my concern of the moment. I know there is something there because of the shadow of worry cast over what I am doing, or the sudden depression which does not seem to be connected with the business in hand. Then I sweep the field and scrutinize all I can see in the back of my mind, bringing each flitting shape into the front to declare itself, so that finally I catch the disturbing thought and have a look at it.

It puzzled me that these back-of-my-mind thoughts should have such power to spread an emotional shadow. Time and again I would find one of them filling me with gloomy forebodings and yet, when I had caught it and turned my searchlight upon it, it was but a little thing, a trivial difficulty which I knew quite well how to surmount. I would feel, for instance, a sudden sense of guilt and a sinking of the heart as if I had made some fatal mistake. Then, on turning to observe what had just crossed my mind I would find there, perhaps, a doubt whether the buttons I had just bought really were a good match for my frock. Of course as soon as I caught the idea I could see what it was and recognize its relative importance, so that the emotion which at first surrounded it became impossible, so absurd that I could not believe that I had ever really felt it. Like a traveller in a dark forest, my imagination seemed able to people the unknown with fearsome creatures, malevolent faces and sounds of evil intent, ghouls which vanish only when in the light of his lantern he recognizes them for familiar things, for twisted tree trunks and the creak of branches in the wind.

Two points interested me here: the capacity of my attention to link whatever it saw on to its own experience and give it an address as I gave my desk an address in space and time: and the curious things which happened to any idea which was outside the sweep of my attention, outside the range of relating influence. For in these fringes of my mind ideas seemed liable to be entirely cut off from common sense and able to take to themselves the most fantastic possibilities of evil. Although I could not yet understand how these ghouls came into being I was quite clear that in order to disperse them I must flash my attention upon the darkness, then haul them out of the bushes by the scruff of the neck and make them show up for what they were. I had found it was fatal to be afraid of any skulking thought, for the more I looked the other way the wilder grew my ideas of its terror; it seemed to collect all the other ideas I had ever feared and organize a massing of ghouls behind my back. But if once I would look it in the face it shrank into everyday size and shape, till my fears seemed incredible and ludicrous.

Now I thought that perhaps I could explain in part what it might be which drove me to that narrow focus with which I had tried to face all my life problems. For by narrowing my attention down to a point I no doubt increased my capacity to understand the small part I was actually looking at, but I also increased that dark area outside its concentrated beams, in which ideas might remain unrecognized, and therefore liable to all the fantastic distortion of blind thinking. Thus the more I turned my attention to details in order to save myself by scrupulous care from these monstrous fears of failure which lurked in the wide field, the more terrible the monsters became, and the more terrible they became the more I dared not face them, which alone would have destroyed their power. But there still remained the question of what drove me in the first place to such narrowing of focus.

Certainly the conviction of my own inadequacy and inferiority, with all its attendant ghouls of punishment and damnation, was the monster whose existence I had first guessed at several years earlier when I was trying to find what it was that seemed to be driving me to excessive effort; but at that time, as I did not understand at all how thought worked, and had no terms in which to describe what I felt was happening, I had called it a taskmaster in hell. A little later I had felt it as the conviction that I was a miserable sinner. But as I did not then know why my automatic mind should assume that I was a miserable sinner, I had not known how to stop thinking it. Now, however, I thought that it might be my mistaken technique for dealing with whatever problems had worried me, even from the very earliest years of childhood. For, whenever I felt guilty or worried about something, instead of admitting it and trying to be quite clear about the ways in which I had failed myself, I had turned my face the other way and feverishly tried to expiate my failure by some other activity. So my efforts were concerned with tasks which would compensate for my sins, but my emotions lingered behind me, cringing before the ghouls.

All the same, this idea did not explain everything. This idea of unadmitted thoughts outside the focus of attention explained the persistence and growth of unreasonable fears, but it did not explain what was the original primal fear which had become so distorted.

Then one day I happened to remember a picture that I had drawn when about fifteen, at a time when I was rather unhappy. It was a picture of a dragon, which I drew out of my head and painted, feeling vaguely that it was a symbol of all my troubles. The reason why I chose, all unknowingly, to represent my difficulties in the form of a fearsome beast, instead of trying to talk directly about what worried me, was not that there was no one at hand who would not have been shocked to listen (though this was probably true), but that I could not have talked about them, for I did not know what they were. So, when I drew my dragon, I could not have said at all what it meant, I only knew that I thought it would be fun to have a picture of all that I disliked in myself. For in those days I used to listen to several sermons in every week and took the moral exhortations of a girls' boarding-school rather seriously. Thus my dragon became a picture of my own faults, something I hated, something to be pinned up on the wall to spur me on to struggle against them. But because I did not really know what my dragon meant I had no notion how to fight it. The only weapons I knew about were good resolutions, and these seemed only to give greater power to my enemy. Actually it was not until ten years later, when I followed up that first vague impulse to give concrete expression to my fears by letting my thoughts run freely in written words, that I began to gain any ground over this adversary. It was then, when I discovered by this means what vehemence of thought could lie only just under the surface of a general tranquillity of mood, that I suddenly remembered the dragon and disinterred his picture from amongst my childhood relics.

When I looked at the picture I remembered what my conscious motives for painting it had been, but I decided to try and find out what the picture might have meant to my automatic mind as well. So I sat down with a paper and pencil to write my thoughts:

Dragon, smoking nostrils, fire, 'tongue is a fire' – Fafnir's blood, burning, made Siegfried understand birds' songs, dead, dead snake, dead snakes in the road, smell of death, dead sheep . . . blood, death, the dead dragon, he killed it, plunged the sword in, dead white scales of its belly, it lay on its back, the dead snake in the road, smelt like bad fish, smell of death, bad, bad meat, dragon, smoking dragon, hot smoking blood, something had its throat cut, smoking blood burning like lava, fire and brimstone, dragon, destruction, valley of destruction, valley of the shadow of death, skulls, grinning skulls, little white rabbit skulls on the sand dunes, bones, white bones, skeleton by the stream, dead, a smell, something dead, dragon, killing, dead, disintegration, why did I draw death? the pit, blackness, swallowed up, swallowed, they said a snake could swallow a goat, dragon, filthy, loathsome, Loathly Worm of Spindlestone, loathly, a toad in the castle well – the dragon had a shield in my drawing, shield, school badge, a shield, Galashiels, why? shiels, sheels, shields, a silver shiels, knights wore them, knighthood, Galahad, how I hated him, Watts made his hair look like a wig, so soppy, shields, a purple shield, purple sky, star, star on it, dragon, Fafnir, coiling body, scales, so inhumanly alive, Fafnir, smoking blood, had I read the *Nibelungenlied* then? Yes, there was a picture in 'Told by the Northmen', also one of Hades, shades, dead things, ghosts, was it death I was fighting? blackness, loss of self, Hecate, Goddess of the underworld, dragon, drag on, drag, plodding on, plod, sod, God, rod, tod, toad, loathly toad.

Even when I had written this I could not see the obvious nature of the symbolism. All I remembered was that this dragon theme had come up again in more recent years. So I looked up in my diary to see whether I could not find a further clue:

Last night in bed I felt a panic fear of death, the loneliness and emptiness. I had an impulse to turn to mother or R. D. for security but knew there was no help in that, there was no help anyway. I couldn't believe in anything after death – only the worm-eaten skull of the Indian chief at the Museum. Why do they say death is beautiful? Because they believe in immortality? A. was happy but then he believed 'underneath are the everlasting arms'. I don't. For me there is nothing and I must face it. Is this the final ordeal of escape from the egocentricity of blind thought? When one's own thought is the universe, extinction is horribly unthinkable. When oneself is recognized as a microbe and one's sympathies are with the whole, does it matter so much? I escaped from the horror which would not let me sleep by the thought of N. [aged ten months] in his little woolly cap. – The men who saw death in the war, how did they cope with it? – In my mind was a vague picture of an Indian wooden fish, a whale? its jaws painted red and green, Jonah and the whale, a dragon, Fafnir, the jaws of death.

Jaws of death. What did that mean? At first I had seen it only in terms of a literal death, forgetting that the ideas of my automatic self were nearly always meta-phorical. Then I began to see it as a fear that my personal identity would be swallowed up and then, gradually, I began to feel sure that it was really this fear which had made me purpose-driven. I felt I had been continually distracted with a life and death issue, I had the desire always to be getting things done to prove to myself that I existed as a person at all. So it was only very rarely that I had felt safe enough to give up striving, particularly as the enemy was really within my own gates. For this urge to let go and let the sea in, which I had discovered when I first set out to explore myself (I was continually dream-ing of being in a town that was threatened by a tidal wave), seemed to be ever driving me on towards in-escapable death. But I could not even yet see the real meaning of this death, and until I did I could not begin to be free of the fear of it. Actually I did not discover what it really meant until I had developed a further technique for finding expression for my outcast thoughts.

CHAPTER XII

More Outcasts of Thought

How can I tell what I think till I see what I say?
Quoted by E. M. FORSTER

THIS study of my dragon picture set me thinking more about the way in which imagined terrors could be brought into the daylight of common sense. When I thought over how I had felt at the time of drawing it I realized again that the fact of certain subjects being taboo was not the only bar to talking out my worries. For the kind of thinking which went on when I was immersed in reverie, when myself and my thought were inextricably merged together, was liable to be so fantastic that it was quite incommunicable. Also, although I had first come to observe the 'back of my mind' thoughts as a kind of silent chatter I gradually found that many of them were even more difficult to observe, for they were not in the form of words at all but consisted of a confusion of feelings and fragmentary images. It was like a dream which immediately eludes you the moment you try to describe it. You say, 'So-and-so came down the street but it was not really she, it might have been my sister as well; I met her in the street, but at the same time we were in an upstairs room – and then I was all by myself'. And all the time you have the feeling that words are quite incapable of conveying the actual experience of the dream; since it seems to take no account of logic, one person can be several different people all at once, a room can be both upstairs and down in the street at the same time.

But if my thought must remain childish and therefore distorted if it was unexpressed, and yet if in its childish form it was too confused and pictorial to be directly expressed, what was to be done? The solution of this difficulty only gradually dawned on me after pondering over what I had at first looked upon simply as meaningless tricks of the imagination. For gradually I became convinced that my outcast thoughts were in fact seeking expression for themselves, quite apart from any effort of mine, but that they could find only an indirect and symbolic language in which to clothe themselves.

The first hint of this came quite accidentally. For a long time I had thought that a good way of getting out of the habit of assuming that an opinion or idea had an absolute value was to be continually looking for the opposite of every statement. One day while I was travelling into the country to stay with a friend I pondered on the possible value of this method and tried to put it into practice. It was rather difficult, however, and after a little while I went on to think of other things. When I reached the end of my journey and was shown my room, I noticed vaguely that there was a colour print of Blake's on the wall, but it was one that I had seen before, so I only gave it a passing glance before going to bed. When I opened my eyes in the morning I found I was looking directly at the picture of a drunken clown peering down from the clouds, with wisps of red hair falling about his besotted face and immense false nose. For a moment I stared in bewilderment, only half awake; than in a flash I remembered the Blake print and at once saw that it was not a drunken clown bending down from the clouds, but God.

My first thought was of the 'opposites' trick. It occurred to me that my mind must have taken the hint; for here it was, at the first opportunity when it could make its voice heard above the drive and clatter of fully awakened thought, showing me the direct opposite of one of my familiar patterns of feeling. For I had always consciously looked on this picture with a certain awe and reverence. Although I had forgotten or perhaps had never known that its title was 'The Ancient of Days', I had always been greatly impressed with the grandeur of the conception. As usual, however, I had given no expression to this feeling. I had accepted it without question, never reflecting that it was but one pattern of thinking, its very existence implying the possibility of its opposite. For the opposite view of the ultimate foundation of the universe was one which I had usually edged away from. Cynical interpretations of life which included the idea of complete absence of plan, or even the idea of malevolent intention at the basis of all existence, had always seemed to me rather far-fetched. I had not, however, carefully reflected whether such views might not be true after all; I had not repudiated them because I considered they were inadequate as an explanation in the light of the facts as I saw them, I had simply brushed them aside. Once only had I really tried to bring such an attitude into the daylight, once when a few weeks before, feeling in despair about my enterprise, I had written:

My discoveries are meaningless, life is just as the cynical see it, something to be borne and forgotten as much as possible, with the help of drugs: drink, noise and hilarity. Trying to find ways of understanding it as I am doing is only fit for adolescents.

But as soon as I had written it I had turned my thoughts away from such an idea and immediately forgotten it. Now, however, I was finding a dramatic example of my recent realization that no idea can be safely shut out of the mind, least of all those that the deliberate self would like to disparage. It seemed that my intention to look for 'opposites', combined with the chance clothing in concrete form offered by the Blake picture, had given the cynical view of life a chance to emerge from its banishment in the dark hinterland of my preoccupations. At once it occurred to me that my mis-seeing of this picture might be symbolic of a fear which had dominated my occasional moods of black despair and hatred against the universe. For my habitual mood was optimistic; and as I had not yet learnt the truth of opposites I was continually turning my face away from all gloomy possibilities, and picturing how I would like things to happen, never thinking what the worst might be. Then when fatigue or some set-back, often only a casual remark or chance incident, caused a weakening or break in the consistency of the cheerful pattern, I would be faced with a rush of forebodings, the gloomy partners of all my past hopes. This would cause such a reversal of mood that I was then quite able to believe the world's events to be caused by the whims of a drunken clown.

Such was the explanation I gave to myself at the time. The full meaning of the symbolism did not occur to me until much later.

I then began to observe other examples of this sudden emergence of a theme directly opposite in mood from that which had been dominating my mind. Particularly did this swing of irreconcilables seem to occur between the sacred and the profane, the reverent and the ribald. I noticed it in dreams as well as in waking life. Here is a dream which I recorded because it had a peculiarly haunting quality:

PART I. – I was in a dark high wood, lofty pines, with people all about in the shadows, waiting. All at once a murmur spread around me, carrying fear. 'The White Grebe!' they said, 'The White Grebe!' and all of them cowered farther down into the shadows, waiting in terror. But I could not hide, I knew that something was coming for me and I was left alone in the great space of the wood. Then I saw a white bird like a heron circling down from the high trees and I knelt down with my hands outstretched, holding my heart in the palms of my hands. Then the bird came and settled on my heart and dug its claws in, but I felt this as a ring of pain about my head, as a crown of thorns. Then I thought of the bird as a Phoenix, a bird of gold that must burn itself to ashes to revive its life.

PART II. – Someone said a white dove had flown round at some Papal gathering, flying to a woman. 'Most appropriate!' they said, with a knowing leer.

The mood of the second part was quite definitely in opposition, for in the first I had been filled with awe, and waiting in breathless humility; in the second the account of the dove's flight was given in that tone of smug cynicism which I associated with cheap journalism.

Then I noticed another example. I was one day deliberately considering the problem of concentration, meditating on the fact that my thought so often refused to go where I wished it and insisted on taking its own path. It had occurred to me that I had in the past always assumed this wilfulness of my thought to be a sheer irrelevance, for on realizing that I was not thinking about what I had set out to think of I would sigh, 'There you go again, wandering thoughts!' and try to whip my mind back on to the path I had chosen. Then I had begun to wonder whether my truant mind might not possess a wisdom of its own, whether it might be worth enquiring what it had been heading for, since so often when I did manage, with tremendous effort, to keep my mind on a chosen subject, I had the feeling that there was something else urgently waiting for attention. While thinking of this there occurred to me the phrase 'Who's that knocking a the door?' as a suggestive analogy for the process. For a moment I accepted the idea without scrutiny, then suddenly noticed that while I had mentally sung the phrase to the tune of 'Barnacle Bill the Sailor' I had had a simultaneous picture of Holman Hunt's 'Light of the World'.

Such discoveries gave me plenty to think about. It seemed so obvious, once I considered it, that every pattern of thought must have its reverse side, that it puzzled me why I found it so hard to turn my ideas upside-down just to see what was there. I supposed it was another result of taking them for absolute things. Certainly my inability to do it accounted for my feeling of dismay when the ridiculous sometimes cropped up with a shattering effect on the sublimity of my mood.

Also, it had often puzzled me how, when other people's intimate affairs were the subject of general conversation, they could so easily be made to sound laughable, obscene and cheap. I felt that my own experiences, which sometimes I had thought grand, sublime, would sound just as bad if mentioned. I could imagine just how they would tell about them. So, when anything important happened to me I told nobody. But perhaps my experiences were really cheap too, and my sense of their importance might be only another ramification of egoism? For the people who talked like this, reducing everything to absurdity, were people I liked, people full of generosity in their acts, not purposely malicious. Not until I understood a little of the nature of thought and the need to be always aware of the obverse of my pattern did I learn to escape this conflict. I saw that to see only the ridiculousness of humanity was just as misleading as to see only its dignity, that what one said or thought about a thing must always be a distortion, that the mistake was to believe that any one expression could be the last word, for experience was always bigger than the formula. It was not that other people's experience was sordid and obscene, mine sacred and marvellous, for theirs to them might be the same as mine to me, and mine to an observer as much a source of merriment. If only I could remember to distinguish the formulation from the fact, and not assume that because it was said it must be true, then I would be able to know that their laughter did not always prove me futile.

. All this was so obvious when I stated it, yet my submerged thought seemed quite incapable of believing it.

And as long as I took the formula for the fact I was at the mercy not only of other people's flippancies, but of my own. All the time, behind the sense of the fullness of my own experience, there seemed to be a dim awareness of the reverse of this. I, who had so often kept silence for fear that others might scoff, found a scoffer within myself whose laughs were just loud enough to cast a shadow of anxiety over my delights.

I observed another aspect of this in my attitude to people. I was always wanting people to be either all lovable or all hateful. When I was getting on well with someone everything they said was right and nothing was too good for them. Then, if some chance altered the emotional situation between us, they would become hateful to me, I would see all their weak points and fail to remember that they had ever had any good ones at all. And it was only by recognizing my thought as thought that I could remember to look deliberately for the reverse side, and remember to express it, so that I could widen my attention enough to view the irreconcilable opposites both together. And only by so doing was I able to realize that neither extreme could represent all the facts; and only when I had seen this could I make a third pattern embodying what was useful in both, but based on discrimination, not on the 'all-or-none' habit of my blind thinking.

Here then was a further light on the inhabitants of those parts of my mind which were still unexplored jungle. Not only were there herds of the special experiences which I had found too unpleasant to think about, but there were also the reversed shadows of every idea I had entertained and accepted with uncritical enthusiasm. For each thought which I kept domesticated and rational in my garden there might be a wild mate lurking outside the walls and howling at nights. But how was I to bring them in, how entice them into the taming influence of my awareness? I had found it was not so easy to catch the reverse of my thought just by wanting to, so here again I had to devise special methods for ensnaring them. One of these was to keep an 'opposites' note-book in which I would from time to time select some attitude or opinion which seemed important to me, and deliberately consider its opposite; for instance, if I was in love I would explore the feelings of indifference, if I was enthusiastic for a particular opinion I would make a list of all there was to be said against it.

In spite of the difficulty of deliberately reversing my thoughts, however, I had by now plenty of evidence that these wild things actually wanted to come in; they often made dumb overtures of friendliness which I, in my terror, failed to recognize. I, whose deliberate thoughts were inclined to be scientific and rational, began to observe strange fragmentary images which had a surprising legendary quality. One day, for instance, when just about to settle myself on the pillion seat of a motor-bicycle, I chanced to look up and caught an instantaneous glimpse of some celestial creature, breathing fire and looming down upon me; but it was only a cart-horse plodding soberly along the road against the sun.

These tricks of my imagination puzzled me. I was not given to dreaming of fabulous happenings, I had not read fairy tales for years and stories of fantasy written for adults rather bored me. But it seemed I only had to scratch the surface of my thinking in order to slip through to mythological levels. One day I thought it would be amusing to draw a map of my life, to show in pictures what I felt had been the most important things in it. I let my mental eye roam over all the happenings, places and situations of my upbringing, and if any had a peculiar quality of emotional significance I tried to represent it in a diagrammatic drawing. I simply followed my impulse and drew unquestioningly what I felt to be important. Then I found that part of my map contained a drawing of a little hill near the town in which I had lived as a child. On top of the hill there was a ruined chapel and at the foot of it was the river crossed by a ferry-boat. I drew this, simply remembering the position of the hill and the river, but as I put in the ferry boat I suddenly thought that this was not the friendly and familiar Wey, or the young ferryman I remembered, but a very different river. For I knew I was drawing a picture of Charon crossing the Styx. This idea surprised me. I knew practically nothing of classical literature; I had learnt a little Latin at school but had given it up after a few years. I vaguely remembered reading the story of Charon in Virgil (or was it Ovid?), but had never thought of it again from that day to this. When I began to wonder why the familiar river of my childhood had become the Styx, I at once remembered how the side of the hill fell precipitously down to the river-bank, how the sandy soil was continually crumbling away and the towpath was here at a dangerous angle from the effect of little landslides. We children were often warned about its dangers and I remembered how black the water was when I looked down across the slope of yellow sand. Apparently, then, my mind had all on its own account woven a pattern out of my childish ideas of death and clothed these in a medley of images drawn indiscriminately from my actual experience and from later casual acquaintance with ancient myth.

As I went on with my drawing I noted more examples of how, at this level of thinking, an idea could be both itself and several other things at the same time. I found once

again that this part of my mind had quite different attitudes from those that my deliberate self had assumed. I had thought of that ruined chapel as a draughty place full of smells and nettles, and never remembered being particularly impressed by it; yet while trying to draw it for my map I had a feeling of its immense significance. Then, being now on the alert for ideas possessing this composite quality, I saw that I was also drawing the Chapel Perilous from *Morte d'Arthur*, although I could not remember a single fact about the Chapel in the story. And on the side of the hill I felt impelled to draw a little spring that used to bubble out from the sandstone and was a great joy to us children since it was the only place we knew of where we were allowed to drink from a stream. In drawing it I felt impelled to put a little dot in the centre of the clear pool into which the water fell, and this, I told myself, was Odin's eye, which he had to give up to somebody in payment for something he wanted. It was also the bent pin I had seen lying at the bottom of a wishing well somewhere in Cornwall. But it would take far too long to go into all the wealth of imagery this drawing aroused, connexions with later reading about fertility rites, ideas of water in a waste place, Moses striking the rock – images which I came to see were all pointing towards an underlying need of which I had not allowed myself to be fully aware.

At this time, however, what particularly interested me was the way in which my thought took to itself material from anywhere and everywhere in order to find a form in which to become clothed and visible. I remembered controversies I had heard about whether reading fairy tales and legends was not a waste of time for children, since they would have their work cut out anyway to discover what were the facts of the world, without having the issue confused with fantasy. But I thought now that it was not only facts about the world that they needed to know, they needed also facts about themselves, and it was only through the imaginative symbols of fantasy that they could at first express their knowledge of themselves. For I began to realize to what a great extent this play of images had provided an indication of what were my true needs. Particularly did I try to make use of dreams in this way.

It was only occasionally, however, that I could guess at any definite meaning in my dreams. For instance, the White Grebe dream interested me first because of the conflict of mood, ecstatic self-surrender followed by scoffing comment, but I had no idea what it meant. Then I happened to tell it to someone, who said at once, 'It meant you wanted a child.' This interpretation had never occurred to me, but as soon as it was mentioned I remembered how the day before the dream it had flashed into my mind, 'Oh, if I had a baby, that would be the end of doing what I like; I would always be having to jump up and do things, wash nappies, be punctual.'

After a time I learnt how to explore for myself dreams that felt emotionally important. I learnt how, while writing down the dream, to record also the first trains of thought which thrust themselves into my mind while I wrote. Here are some such associations to the bare story of the White Grebe dream:

PHOENIX. He that saveth his life ... except a grain of wheat ...

GREBE. Soft feathers, the pelican that plucks its own, also its heart ... the stork, bringing children. ... At some church in Italy it is said that the women bring white doves to a certain festival under their cloaks and let them fly in the middle of the service.

WHITE. The whiteness of the whale (Moby Dick) evil, negation, terror of annihilation.

According to my diary these associations were written when I recorded the rest of the dream, and two days before I told it to anyone and was given the interpretation mentioned above. But it puzzles me a little that I could have failed to see for myself the suggested central theme. I suppose I must have guessed that it referred to some sacrifice that I might be demanding of myself, but I had failed to interpret it in specific terms because I did not really want to face the problem.

In another dream I experienced feelings immediately arousing thoughts of birth and this was before I had discovered, through reading, that so-called 'birth dreams' are very common:

– going down on a tram that went through a tunnel, the lines going almost vertically down – I thought, supposing the brakes gave way! and then a fear of being swallowed up, and a picture of the wolves that swallowed the sun, swallowed the chariot of the Sun God, Balder, Apollo.

At the time I could not see any reason for the dream at all, but afterwards guessed that it might refer to the beginning of a new life, since it occurred at the time of my first indecisions about possible ways to cure my own discontent (Chapter I, p. 24).

I observed also certain recurring themes in my dreaming. One, which I have already noted, was of being overwhelmed by a tidal wave. I mention this particularly because it was a theme which eventually pushed its way into expression through drawing, This happened one day when I was trying, just for amusement, to work out the design for an illustration to the lines:

> Whenever the moon and the stars are set,
>   Whenever the wind is high,
> All night long in the dark and the wet,
>   A man goes riding by.

I had planned in detail a figure of the horseman but felt the need for a simple form of lines to give the right mood, and began experimenting with sweeping curves. (This was the first time I had tried illustrating in this way.) Here is what I drew:

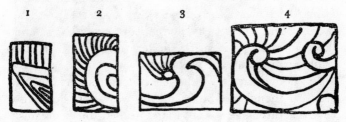

5

6

7

Actually I never made the picture I had planned, for the designs did not seem to be just what I wanted, they had some quality which did not please me. So I gave up, deciding that I was probably not a born illustrator. But the designs remained in my drawing-book. Several years later, when I began the map of my life to which I have already referred, I remembered my tidal-wave dream, and, feeling it stood for something important, cast about for ways of representing it. At once these old designs came to my mind and it seemed to me that Fig. 6 was certainly a tidal wave. My mind jumped to the thought that it stood for the panic dread of being overwhelmed by the boundless sea of what was not myself.

But this did not seem to be the end of the significance of those designs. For as I felt back into my childhood to fill in the earlier parts of my map I found a looming fear of thunder, and when I searched for ways of drawing this these designs again came into my mind (Fig. 7). The building shown on the hill-top is partly associated with St Martha's chapel which crowns the Pilgrim's Way, a place which I came to know only later, and partly connected with a hymn we used to sing as children:

> There is a green hill far away,
> Without a city wall.

I did not know why I was impelled to draw St Martha's in the picture, but the meaning of the little knob on the left was clear to me. It was the electrical machine in my father's study (p. 61) which gave sparks. Now I felt certain that the map represented the whole complex of associated ideas linking thunder with thoughts of parental and divine anger, of guilt and primitive fear and my own emotional urges.

*

When I had first started free writing as an experiment (Chapter III) I had been forced to realize that my mind had thoughts I did not know about. Now I was being made to recognize that without any doubt I also had needs which might be quite different from those my everyday conscious self regarded as important. At first I had not known at all how to distinguish between things that I thought I ought to want because other people did, and those that were fundamentally appropriate to my own situation and nature. I had been very much inclined to intellectualize my wants, to try to decide what it might be good to want and then assume that I did want it; and I noticed that my friends did this too. They would, for example, decide that jealousy was not a noble emotion and then imagine that this was enough to prevent them feeling it; so they would let the most impossible situations develop and then be surprised to find themselves suddenly gushing out hatred. I thought my desire for a baby was also an example of this. Of course I had known that I would very much like to have one. I had certainly put it on my list of wants. But I had been inclined to look upon it as a subject for reasonable discussion, something that could be decided upon the basis of intellectually balanced pros and cons, a matter of convenience and the exact state of one's income. It was not until I discovered how needs perhaps quite unsuspected by me seemed to be striving to make themselves known, that I saw the matter in quite a different light. I saw it then as an imperious demand which, for me at least, if denied by an arrogant intellect, had power to take its revenge in quite unguessed-at ways. In fact, so great was the conflict, that even after I had actually fulfilled this need my intellect continued to play tricks with me, and I quite failed to recognize the obvious physiological signs of what was happening. When I did finally understand, my angel of annunciation came upon me when I was one day walking along a sheep-trodden winding path. I suddenly found myself standing quite still, gazing down at a pattern of little hoof-marks in the sun-baked mud – and a flood of contentment welled up from beneath my feet.

In spite of all this, I could not understand why such an obvious and universal need could also be a blinding terror.

CHAPTER XIII

Relaxing

We are great fools. 'He has passed over his life in idleness,' say we: 'I have done nothing to-day.' What? Have you not lived? That is not only the fundamental, but the most illustrious of all your occupations. 'Had I been put to the management of great affairs, I should have made it seen what I could do.' Have you known how to meditate and manage your life, you have performed the greatest work oı all. For a man to show and set out himself, nature has no need of fortune; she equally manifests herself in all stages, and behind a curtain as well as without one. Have you known how to regulate your conduct, you have done a great deal more than he who has composed books. Have you known how to take repose, you have done more than he who has taken cities and empires.

MONTAIGNE

As a result of these discoveries moods became more under my own control. But not entirely so by any means. For there were times when, although I thought myself free from any distracting anxiety or obsessive longing, my thoughts still made a chattering barrier between me and what I wanted to experience. There were times when I was neither tense with anticipation nor anxious over half-glimpsed difficulties, but was still, for some reason, unable to emerge into wide looking. It usually happened, not before, but after any excitement, particularly at night, or at the beginning of a holiday. Then, when I was hoping for nothing but sleep and peace, the chattering echoes of recent concerns would race through my head, and the more I sought rest the more I could not find it.

It seemed that after any excitement my thoughts carried on with such a momentum of their own that the gesture of standing aside was not enough to still them. One day, however, I was taught a new technique, a trick considered valuable for the health of the body but which I soon found had immeasurable effects upon the mind as well. I was shown how to relax all the muscles of my body deliberately.

There were many different ways of doing it. In all of them the first essential seemed to be to lie flat on one's back. Later, when I made the habit of always deliberately relaxing before going to sleep, I used often to feel inclined to evade this condition, to argue that surely I could do it just as well on my side when curled up ready for sleep. But it did not do just as well; if I gave in to the impulses I would wake up to remember a night of tossing restlessness.

Once flat on one's back the next step varied. One method, advised by a doctor, was to shut your eyes, and raising up the left arm, fully outstretched, o let it sink down as slowly as possible till it gradually reached the bed and fell as 'limp as a tassel' at your side. According to the instructions, the rest of the body automatically responds to the limpness of the arm. I certainly found this method worked well, but there were others which sometimes worked better. For when my thoughts were specially boisterous they sometimes seemed actually to prevent the automatic response of the rest of my body to the arm's repose. So at these times I found that methods which gave the mind something to do as well were more effective. For instance, it was possible to make a mental gesture of withdrawing all the energy from one's limbs. Still another way, which I discovered for myself, was to imagine the sensations of massage. A modification of this, particularly useful when there was not very much time, was to stroke one's own eyelids in imagination with the tips of one's fingers, carrying the movement all up and down the back of the ears and over the scalp, doing in imagination what the hairdressers say is good for the hair.

Complete relaxing never happened all at once. I found that it was a matter of at least five or ten minutes before the body would reach a profound repose. So I made a rule for myself, that as long as I felt an impulse to get up or turn over, then I had not lain long enough, but as soon as I felt I never wanted to move again, then it was all right to get up at once. But I usually did not, I lay still for a little longer, lay still while all the cells of my body came alive, like parched earth after rain. And then I discovered the most fitting end to my rest – a long cat-like stretch, which leaves one so at peace with the world, smooth and shining like wet sands, that it is worth indulging in deliberately, even when not prompted by a natural impulse.

The attempt to understand the art of relaxing taught me many things about the effects of mind on body and body on mind. I had long ago found that my mental gesture of standing aside brought an automatic easing of bodily tensions. I had sometimes found that it was enough simply to take control of my own thoughts, even to repeat over and over some jingle of words, and at once I would find myself taking deeper breaths and moving more freely. Why, when I said: 'I wish I were a cassowary, on the plains of Timbuctoo' over and over to myself, did the colour and shape of my surroundings leap into realness, just as when I made my mental gesture of standing aside? And it happened not only with objects but with people. Sitting tired and bored, staring at a row of dim people in a train, I had only to gabble some nonsense, and each one became a unique thing, his essential character shining out from his very boots. The results were just the same as when I had discovered that I could, by a mental act, place my centre of awareness where I chose. Now, however, I was discovering that I could bring about the same mental effect by simply attending to the relaxing of my muscles. Brooding over this, I began to see how it fitted into my earlier ideas. I saw that for me at last, since to 'let go', to be mentally passive, meant to be driven by effort, it was only by being mentally active that I could really relax. It was a kind of 'diligent indolence' and it did not matter whether it was concerned with my thoughts or with my muscles. People had often told me to 'let go' more, to give myself up to music or impulse, or rest, and I had always thought it meant a passive plunging into the oblivion of my blind thought. But always, when given its head, my blind thought had carried me away into hot, fussy anxieties or long-winded scheming for things it wanted, some plan or other which would not let me rest. And this state had spread from my mind to my body, so that my muscles were always taut with the effort to get what I wanted. Now, however, when I had at last learnt the restraining act which was real 'letting go', the chatter of blind effortful thought dwindled from an exhausting distraction to the far-away twitter of sparrows high up in the eaves.

I soon found that knowing how to relax had other advantages besides improving my rest and my powers of perception. For instance, it acted like magic on those floods of irritation which are sometimes provoked by a particular person, an insistent mannerism, or some repeated distracting noise. Instead of narrowing my will to a fine point of exasperation – 'Oh, why won't they stop it' – I found that I could relax towards the distraction; instead of trying to push it away I could open my arms to it and let it do its worst. I found that even pain could be made bearable by this. I could also treat particular difficulties in my work in the same way. It was a long time since I had first observed my mind's habit of tightening and narrowing its energies when there was any hitch in the progress of my thought, but now I was finding that the deliberate relaxing of my muscles was one way of achieving that mental gesture of standing aside from a problem which I had found so essential. Gradually I learnt how to remain unmoved against the flood of panic impulses which tried to rush me into greater effort at the first hint of difficulty with a clamouring chorus of, 'Oh, that is all wrong, all on the wrong tack – I'll never get it done in time – I ought never to have started – but now I'm in for it I must try, try, try'.

I was also astonished to find the effect of relaxing upon physical skill. Just as I had begun this whole enterprise thinking that the critical point would lie in what I did, and that looking at the facts was only a preliminary before deciding what to do, so in skilled movements I had thought success depended upon the direct willing of the movement. And just as I had found out that in the management of my life to see the facts was not a preliminary excursion but the very core of the problem, for what I did followed inevitably on what I had seen, so I found quite a new approach to the question of skill. I found that if I used my will to keep my attention fixed on the end I wanted to achieve and on keeping my muscles relaxed, then the body knew how to find its own means, I did not have to think about what my limbs were doing at all. If I did try to manage my muscles deliberately I was merely interfering in a job that my body knew much better how to manage than I did. For instance, I had never been particularly good at games. Quite suddenly, however, while playing clock-golf one summer evening I found that time after time I could reach the hole in one shot. Trying to observe what this change from my usual style seemed due to, I found that I was thinking of nothing but the hole, I was keeping my mind fixed on that and never giving a thought to what I did with my club. Something similar happened in tennis. I had had many rules which I had always tried to keep in mind, with no very marked success – to stand firm on my feet and sideways to the net when taking a ball, to 'follow through' with my racket, to keep my eye on the ball and the head of my racket up. But I never managed to re-member all at once, and one day it occurred to me to keep my mind only on the two ideas of an absolutely re-laxed body and the place where I wished the ball to go. Here again right 'doing' seemed to follow automatically from seeing what was to be done; it needed no special effort of its own.

After such discoveries I found that these were par-ticular instances of a well-recognized mental law.* I found it even applied to clumsiness about the house. Be-fore, as soon as anything had to be done carefully, I would try to force my actual muscular movements and then find that my fingers became all thumbs. I could now under-stand what had happened when I first found out how to stand aside when darning stockings, for I was really at-tending to the watching of my movements instead of to the pushing of them.

I then discovered two more applications of the same principle. One was when trying to draw animals at the Zoo. I had begun in my usual way, trying to control the movement of my hand deliberately, drawing anxious and cautious lines, slowly, in order to be sure of getting it

*Law of reversed effort. C. Baudouin, *Suggestion and Auto-Suggestion*.

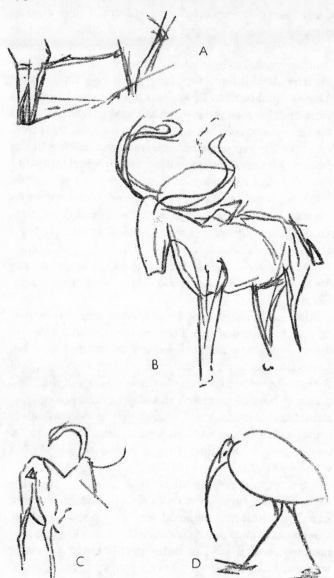

right, sadly, because I felt all the time, 'Oh dear, I'm
sure that's wrong, he's going to look more like a fat pig,
and he's really such a gorgeous beast; oh, and now he's
going to move before I've half finished.' The result was
Figure A, and it had taken me quite a long time to produce even that much. I was just turning away in despair,
determined to give up drawing as a too depressing hobby,
when I chanced to look up and saw that the creature I
was drawing had posed himself upon the rocks, and the
shape of him so seized hold of me that there was no room
for thought of my own incapacity, I just began to draw
in frantic haste. In a quarter of the time spent on the first
attempt I had at least mapped in the essentials of what
had caught my fancy (Figure B) before he moved away
again.

This had been a spontaneous self-forgetting when the
chance interest of a shape had lifted me out of my care-
fulness. Now, however, I tried to repeat the experience
deliberately by holding my attention on what I was looking at, and deliberately forgetting my hand and my
drawing (Figure C). Again the creature moved away before I had half begun; but then I decided to try on something that was moving all the time, so when I caught a
glimpse of a long-legged bird I turned my glance away at
once in order that the first impression should not be confused. Then I kept my attention fixed on this mental
image, and let my hand draw as it would. I wondered
why I had been so long in finding out that to go carefully
was not necessarily to go as I wished.

My second application concerned singing. As a child
I had been teased for singing out of tune and so all my
life I had felt stupid and thwarted, ashamed to burst into
song whenever I felt like it and deeply envious of those
who could. I could always hear when other people were

out of tune but seemed incapable of producing true notes myself. Then one day I happened to start humming without thinking about it, for there was no one close enough to overhear, and I suddenly listened to my own voice and heard that it was in tune. I was so interested that I went on listening, and as long as I listened, so long did I stay in tune. But as soon as my attention slipped back to the problem of trying to sing, then my voice wandered off the note. It seemed that I had always tried to keep in tune by attending to the muscles in my throat which felt as if they controlled the sound, just as I had tried to play tennis by the deliberate placing of my limbs. After this I found that I could keep in tune whenever I chose, so long as I thought only of the melody and forgot that my throat existed.

I next began to realize that not only must I not try to drive my muscles, but also I must not try to drive my sensations. I found that if, when I was wanting to perceive, I stood back and let my eye take its own course it had many things to tell me. I had had my first hint of this in the Black Forest, but I had not then understood how to stand back and wait. Now I was finding that my eye had quite definite interests of its own, that when it was not driven into being the slave of my desires, or browbeaten into providing me with information, it liked looking at things for their own sake and saw quite a different world. It saw, for instance, that shapes and lines have movement. For one day I began staring at one of those iron grids where the heated air comes into a room; my busy mind of course knew it was there but had been too hurried to do more than give it a passing glance as 'that old iron thing'. But now, when completely relaxed and idly staring, my eye found delight in it. I found myself looking first at one side, then at the other – they were symmetrical curves with a pillar in the centre and radiating lines thrusting downward like the cloak of a queen – and as I watched, the form seemed to crystallize under my eye into a growing equilibrium of movement. Now I knew what painters meant about the movement of lines. If one only stood still and watched, they did move. And I thought I understood what being blind to ugliness meant. It meant that the eye was enslaved to thought, and that one was valuing things for what they made one think of, not for their own sakes.

There were also other more general results. The automatic widening of mental focus which seemed to follow muscular relaxing brought a twofold deepening of experience, a flooding in of overtones both from present bodily awareness and also from the past, in wave after wave of memories. It was not that I turned away from the present in order to think of the past but that the past gave added richness to the present. When going my ways with contracted body and narrow focused mind I always felt I was missing things, a feeling of the glory that had departed or that belonged to someone else. Spring was never what it used to be; if only I were somewhere else perhaps it would be better; and I would plunge into aching envy of others who were where I would like to be, in the country, beside the Mediterranean, looking at mountains. But whenever I could remember to relax, then the glory of my childhood had not departed, time and place did not matter any more, one sniff of the morning air brought the distilled essence of all my springs. Looking out of a London window, clear sun with a touch of frost, there flooded in to me all the sunlit frosty mornings on still commons, with little panes of crackling ice in the horses' hoof-marks. And again, one day in the Luxembourg gardens when narrow focus had made me feel tiresomely uneducated, wishing I knew some history so that I could understand more about what I was seeing, I remembered to relax; at once I knew that I needed no history in order to understand what the races of men had felt about fountains.

Experiencing the present with the whole of my body instead of with the pin-point of my intellect led to all sorts of new knowledge and new contentment. I began to guess what it might mean to live from the heart instead of the head, and I began to feel movements of the heart which told me more surely what I wanted than any making of lists. And since what filled my mind when I was relaxed flowed out so easily into action, I began to see all sorts of possibilities in the effect of deliberate and controlled imaginations.

CHAPTER XIV

Cart-Horse or Pegasus?

It was a little before the great rains, just now mentioned, that I threw all this stuff away, taking no notice of anything and not so much remembering that I had thrown anything there; when, about a month after or thereabouts, I saw some few stalks of something green shooting up on the ground, which I fancied might be some plant I had not seen; but I was surprised and perfectly astonished, when, after a little longer time, I saw about ten or twelve ears come out, which were perfect green barley. . . .

                                        DANIEL DEFOE

I HAD now learnt the advantages of deliberate relaxing. My next task was to find out what this had to do with my habitual attitudes. I had already been forced to realize the importance of making my thought see itself, but I had also become fully aware of the difficulties of this process. For I could not always be writing my thoughts, or spend all day talking out my blind desires to someone who could give them back to me afterwards in their true light and point out to me the absurdities of what I had said. So I set out to find a moment to moment technique, some way by which in ordinary times, when I was neither overtired nor emotionally wrought-up, I could still make sure of not slipping into all the mistakes and contractions of blind thinking.

I had read somewhere an exhortation to 'continual mindfulness' and for years I had been trying to attain this, thinking that the best way would be, whenever I was doing semi-automatic work which needed no attention, to keep the mind on a particular self-chosen subject. So I would begin, just as when I had once tried formal exercises in concentrating, full of determination to push my thought forward and find ideas in the subject I had selected. And always after a minute or two, probably a few seconds only, I would be exasperated to find I was thinking of something quite different.

Then one day it occurred to me to wonder whether this continual mindfulness in the sense I had imagined it was really possible at all. For I could not help observing that there was some sort of regularity about my lapses. I remembered experiments I had heard of on the natural oscillations of attention, as if this bright pin-point of clear awareness were quickly tired, so that there must be a regular sinking into oblivion for a momentary recovery. I began to suspect that there might be a rhythm of thinking just as there is a rhythm of the heart-beat, and I perhaps had been concerning myself with one phase only, trying to make the strong push forward last all the time, never recognizing the need to stand aside for the inflow. So each time I 'came-to' again after the moment of oblivion I felt I had failed, I did not guess that that moment was just as necessary in the progress of my thought as the other. Often it worried me that I was so bad at thinking out any problem, for I quite often had isolated good ideas but I had no control over them, so I could not arrive at a solution when it was needed; always this moment of oblivion broke the sequence of my thought. Then one day, when I had decided that it was essential I should think about a certain person, and I was just feeling hopelessly aware that I had once more let my thoughts wander on to something else, I happened to glance back and catch a glimpse of where the wandering thought had been. I was astonished to find that it had actually been concerned with the person I wanted to think about, but because it had produced an unexpected aspect of the facts and had not been the result of that kind of self-

conscious thinking I had thought was the only construc-
tive kind, I had dismissed it as irrelevant. This reminded
me of my earlier most important discovery, that I must
watch my thoughts, not push them. It seemed to me now
that I had not been able to make full use of that discovery
before because I had not understood that this watching
must be a rhythmic process; I had not understood that I
could not watch all the time, but that in the moments of
relaxed attention my thoughts could nevertheless get on
by themselves with the job I had set them. What I had
been doing, apparently, was refusing to recognize what
they were offering, beating my ass for not getting on
when all the time it was trying to tell me what I needed
to know.

One morning, when I had been considering this question of how to keep my mind on a definite subject, I woke
up from a dream with the words 'Think backwards, not
forwards', in my mind. At once I recognized this as the
centre of my problem. What I had to do, in the conscious
phase of my thinking, was not to strain forward after new
ideas, but deliberately to look back over the unconscious
phase and see what bearing the ideas there thrown up
had upon the matter in hand. Instead of trying to deal
with wandering thoughts by shamefacedly pretending I
never had any, I must recognize these blind excursions
as an essential part of thought, and always look to them
to decide what they were about. It was here that my
practice in catching 'butterflies' came in useful, for it
helped me to trace back even the more devious reveries.
I found then that one of the troubles had been that I had
not realized how subtle were the little motions of thought.
I had looked for something busier and noisier and failed
to notice what was never more than a little flitting of
birds. It seemed to me that Rodin's 'Le Penseur' well

represented my first idea about thought, for he is making such a to-do about his thinking; but now, for me at least, a more appropriate figure would have been a still watcher in woods.

What I actually found when I did look at the unconscious phase of my thought varied enormously. It was by no means always a contribution to the problem in hand, so I set out to find what conditions its usefulness might depend on. It seemed to be both very obstinate and very docile. Sometimes I had merely to realize the nature of my problem and the answer would be provided without any effort on my part. I would come in to find that the 'Little People' had done my mental housework for me while I was away, and done it better than I could. At other times it would take not the slightest notice of my wishes, it would keep me preoccupied with a futile irrelevancy, some stupidly nagging echoes of a remark someone had made, remembrance of something silly I had done, or worry over trivial details; and it would come back again and again to the annoyance with exasperating persistence. After a long time I came to the conclusion that the nagging thought was always one that was concerned with some unsatisfied emotional need, a need which for some reason I was refusing to recognize and which could not therefore obtain direct expression. By realizing this I then came to be able to make use of these very obstinacies, to use them as a means of finding out what were my own needs. For instance, when I found that my wandering thought was perpetually straying off to the idea of some special person I learnt to suspect two possibilities: either that blind thought had confused that person with someone who was emotionally important to me in the past, probably some member of my own family; or that that person's outstanding quality as I saw him was something that was lacking in myself. Like a cannibal eating his enemy's heart in order to partake of his courage, I was impelled towards someone whose qualities I felt the need of. I could usually tell by my own feelings, by whether the idea 'clicked', which was the true explanation, and if it had seemed to fit, then I found that the obsessive thought no longer drew my attention. I was then able to take into account the need so disclosed, in planning my actions.

It seemed probable, then, that the relevance of the ideas of the unconscious phase to whatever problem I might have in hand depended upon how much I had allowed the subject to become expressed. As far as I could see, those useful ideas which sometimes popped up from the welter of my free drifting thoughts were usually concerned with a subject which I had at some time or other tried to formulate clearly, while the irrelevant or nagging thoughts occurred about subjects which I had never attempted to express because I was afraid or ashamed to think about them. It seemed that my blind thoughts would serve me well, with even magical skill, if I took an interest in their activities, but if I completely ignored them they were liable to get into mischief by slipping into all the irrationalities of the untaught childish state.

Sometimes, when I simply asked: 'What was I thinking?' I would feel as though I had just stopped trying to push with my head down and my eyes shut against an immovable load; all the hot struggling thoughts would die away as I stood aside with a deep breath of relief and cool air in my face. And yet in spite of all this I did not find it easy to do. Whenever I tried to trace back a reverie I felt a strong disinclination, in fact an almost irresistible impulse, to go on pushing. I did not quite understand why this was. Perhaps it was another case of fear of what was outside the beam of clear attention, a general dread of putting things into words for fear of what might be disclosed.

It seemed to be another kind of fear also. For to look back at my thought meant to stop pushing onward; but something in me felt it was not safe to stop. 'If you stop for an instant you'll be lost.' Once I had had a nightmare of trying to cling on to a huge mountain slope by little tufts of grass. I was roped to others and terrified of falling, but eventually I did manage to climb down. I remembered this dream when I was considering my fear of stopping to look at my thought, and I had the idea that this fear of falling was the fear of no-action, the feeling that if I gave up desires, plans, intentions, I would be lost. Occasionally, in clear moments, I could see what I was doing; for instance:

I was full of resentment about my 'rights', saying over and over again to myself, 'It's a shame, he shouldn't let me do it, it's a shame.' Then that phrase came into my mind, 'The separate ego entity is an illusion'; and at once the brooding over my rights, just what he should do and I should do, seemed totally irrelevant. At once I felt clear, transparent, all parts of me smooth, cool-eyed. . . . 'Seeketh not her own.' . . . It's a year since I first had this idea, yet only now is it becoming real. . . . 'Saith not "ego" but doeth it.'* . . . I was afraid there'd be no 'doing' if I did not say 'I', brood over 'I', fight for 'I'. Now I'm letting 'I' go, but eat my breakfast just the same, and it tastes better, for I'm not impelled to hurry to think of something which must be done to save 'I'. So there's nothing

---

*'The body is a big sagacity. An instrument of thy body is also thy little sagacity, my brother, which thou callest "spirit" – a little instrument and plaything of thy big sagacity.

'"Ego" sayest thou, and art proud of that word. But the greater thing – in which thou art unwilling to believe – is thy body with its big sagacity; it saith not "ego", but doeth it.' – NIETZSCHE.

to distract me from the taste of my marmalade and crisp toast.
And I get C.'s breakfast just the same. And as I glance out of
the window I notice an apple tree, black branches against the
white of frost-covered roofs – and it seems much better than
brooding over my rights.

And again:

On the downs above Ashbury, walking past Wayland Smith's
cave. I felt I ought to be thinking about something, getting the
most out of the Downs, and yet constantly preoccupied with
thoughts. Then I said, 'The self in all these things does not know,
it just is. I will sink down into my heart and just be.' Walking
over the thyme on the earthwork slope, for a moment I lost my
personal self. Then I found that I was afraid that if I didn't
think, do something, according to my own little plan, I'd be
lost, sink into a coma of inaction. (There flashed in my mind a
picture of a lunatic I had seen, sitting, all day and always, like
a Buddha.) So I can't sink down and let the tide of my real
being take me, for if I try and for a moment can see no direction, cannot tell where I am going, I am filled with panic,
scared of emptiness. I must be doing something, doing something for my own salvation. . . . The answer to 'What shall I
think about?' then seems to be 'Watch and wait . . . wait
patiently for the Lord', keep still, silent, not only look, but
listen. . . . I tried, walking along the Ridgeway. Soon, instead
of feeling I ought to be in touch with the landscape but
couldn't, I found colours and shapes appearing of themselves.
. . . I began to exult, to see the cornfields and hedges and
downs as exultant. . . . Did the Stone Age people walk this road
exulting? Singing exultant songs? All religion is not dirges and
beseechings, one forgets sometimes. . . .

If the self is what they say it is, surely it does not need my
little plannings and purposes to tell it what to do. But J. F.
chatters so, and is so full of zeal, and the self is not rude, it will
not interrupt.

It struck me as odd that it had taken me so long to
reach a feeling of sureness that there was something in me
that would get on with the job of living without my continual tampering. I suppose I did not really reach it until

I had discovered how to sink down beneath the level of chattering thoughts and simply feel what it meant to be alive. When I had really learnt how to do this, the excessive busyness of my thoughts no longer worried me, at least not as long as I was vigilant enough to prevent blind thinking bolting along its old trails, as long as I remembered the need for that activity which was required to produce inactivity. And once I had made contact with my own source of life, then belief or doubt about 'everlasting arms' was quite irrelevant; just as one does not *believe* that the apple one eats tastes good, it *is* good.

One day the phrase, 'Thy will, not mine, O Lord', rang in my head. I stopped to consider what it might mean.

'Thy' as this insistent reality which comes back at me, wells up from inside, frightens me by its nearness, shocks me by its inclusiveness because it's in the things I love, the lustiness and vigour and lavish things, and abandon – which before I had put aside as outside, not God.

This isolated thought reminded me of some of my earlier experiments of six years ago, and I decided to try again to find what my automatic self thought about God, to see whether blind thinking might perhaps have changed its ideas in the interval:

GOD ... 'of our fathers, known of old', God, God help me, God, not what I'm discovering, not Tao, too near, God, rod, sod, same old things! sod, sodden, drunken sod, looking down from heaven, blessed damosel, warm breast, clown, drunken clown, God, oh God, not you, not anything so near, you are something remote, 'beyond and yet again beyond', but you are not beyond, your eyes laugh, but are sad, brooding, feeling, little mice, furry things, brooding over everything, like a mother chicken, brooding in everything, genesis, the conception, I am the seed, the pattern, the pull and tenseness of the Early Purple

Orchis, the Meadow Crane's Bill, the whirl of a dandelion head seeded, the stresses and strains that keep a plant upright, what else? sex, isn't it that? the dark sea, the dark stream, thoughtless, the apple leaf's becoming, being, not thinking, those horses, they just are, not thought, something upholding things, the tenseness of vitality, the pattern, order, arrangement, precision, you playing, you absorbed, you like a child playing, having your own concerns, beyond me, your own designs, that's the word, design, not purposes or intentions but design, like a drawing, every part holding together, a crispness, a wholeness, precise like a formula, like a dance, a crystal . . . yes, a crystal, forming a pattern out of nothing . . . but isn't this impersonal? but it is your concern, your being, not impersonal really, God, it is not your name, you are too near, God, no, not that. . . .

Apparently, then, this part of my mind had got over some of its fears and hatred in the intervening years, and I thought that this might perhaps be connected with my growing ability to recognize my own unwitting thoughts.

Although by these means I had slowly come to understand some of the ways by which unconscious thoughts could be brought to bear upon conscious problems, there was still a great deal that puzzled me. My greatest ignorance seemed concerned with the weather and seasons of the mind. For although it seemed advisable at all times to look back and formulate what had just passed through my head, there were some moods when even the effort to see the implication of reveries was too great, too purposive, when it seemed that the only thing to do was to hold the mind still and simply accept what came. Occasionally there seemed to be particularly high tides that would throw up at my feet all manner of treasures, oddments which often appeared at first to be isolated ideas whose value I could not see, but which always lured me on to beachcomb regardless of whatever else I ought to have been doing, lured me on to wander along smooth-washed sands. But there were other times when I was perhaps particularly in search of a new idea and I would try to beachcomb, only to find that the tide was out and all the treasures already found or trodden into the sand. So it was very difficult to know just when to leave my thoughts alone and when the effort to express was essential. It always seemed essential in the case of personal thoughts, but there were some ideas which seemed to wither if brought to birth too soon, there were times when I felt a peculiar lassitude and stillness, a need to hold myself suspended till the glowing crucible of my thought was bright enough to fuse the disconnected ideas. Such moods occurred, however, only when I was trying to create something from internal experiences. In perceiving the external world the effort to express what I saw invariably brought rich results. Often, when vaguely bored in a restaurant or the street, it would be enough to say, for instance: 'That man looks like a pig', and at once I would find he had become alive, and that there were endless interesting things to notice about him.

Sometimes, however, both what I noticed and the expression of it would seem to be forced upon me and descend in a shower of delight. For instance:

Grape Harvest beside the Mediterranean.

I came to the beach feeling sick and cold . . . then slowly the waves became a delight, white reflexions on the wet sand, the rhythm with which they follow each other and seep back, the seethe and crispness that I taste on my tongue. So – I inherit the earth . . . then I let the sun and sky and waves possess me and emerged feeling they were part of my being . . . 'conceived by the Holy Ghost' . . . isn't something born of this? Then, coming home through the vineyards to the village, the air full of the smell of grape pulp, breathing it, tasting it, I remembered the Eucharist. . . . One does want to swallow and be swallowed by one's love.

I came to the conclusion then that 'continual mind-fulness' could certainly not mean that my little conscious self should be entirely responsible for marshalling and arranging all my thoughts, for it simply did not know enough. It must mean, not a sergeant-major-like drilling of thoughts, but a continual readiness to look and readiness to accept whatever came. The worst sin, then, was to refuse to accept any thought, for it was only by scrutinizing everything that I could wean my blind thinking away from its childish preoccupations and make it assist in real present-day problems. Certainly whenever I did so manage to win its services I began to suspect that thought, which I had always before looked on as a cart-horse, to be driven, whipped and plodding between shafts, might be really a Pegasus, so suddenly did it alight beside me from places I had no knowledge of.

CHAPTER XV

Discovery of the 'Other'

I cast my eyes to the ship, and there she rode within a little more than half a mile of the shore, for they had weighed her anchor as soon as they were masters of her, and the weather being fair, had brought her to an anchor just against the mouth of a little creek, and the tide being up, the captain had brought the pinnace in near the place where I first landed my rafts, and so landed just at my door.

I was, at first, ready to sink down with surprise, for I saw my deliverance indeed visibly put into my hands, all things easy, and a large ship just ready to carry me away, whither I pleased to go.

DANIEL DEFOE

ALTHOUGH relaxing and watching my thought seemed to have all these advantages, I still had not learnt how to do it continualy. When considering this I ran over in my mind all the occasions on which I had managed to do it, and then I realized that it had always happened when I was alone, for when with other people I seemed to tighten up and make a protective ring between myself and the world.

I remembered how, when I had first discovered that it was possible to spread wide the invisible feelers of mind, to push myself out into the landscape or the movements of a flying bird, I had felt a panic fear. Gradually, however, as I had found that nothing terrible happened, but only great delight, I had apparently lost such feelings and in the world of nature I had begun to feel safe; but apprehension still lurked in my attempts at other kinds of perception. Sometimes in listening to music I would feel myself being carried away until neither I nor anything else existed but only sound, and in spite of the delight I would clutch wildly at some wandering thought to bring me back to the familiar world of bored self-consciousness. Once when listening to a Brahms Quartet I suddenly wanted to gasp out: 'Oh, stop, stop, he shouldn't pour out his heart like that, he'll get hurt. Those are the things one hides.' And then again, in looking at architecture, I discovered fear. I had never been able to find buildings as interesting as pictures, though I felt sure they must be if only I knew how to look. I used to drift round churches with other people, famous places that everyone said ought to be seen and admired, but I always found my attention wandering, always found myself wishing they would get it over quickly and come out in the sun, for my gesture of deliberate wide perceiving never seemed to work here; or perhaps it was that I could never bring myself to try it. Then, one day after I had had some practice in learning how to relax, I was taken to see some sculpture (a form of art which I had always before found rather puzzling). But this time I discovered that by keeping very still and forgetting everything I had been told, I could slip down into a world of dark tensions, stresses and strains that forged themselves into an obscure but deep satisfaction. I felt it in my bones and in my feet and in my breathing. Soon after this I happened to be in Westminster Abbey, a place I had always found vaguely tiresome, hating the litter of monuments and chairs. I was waiting for some music to begin and looked about me, trying to break through the fog of associations and to escape from my preconceived ideas of boredom in churches. Suddenly I succeeded, suddenly I managed to strip my mind clean of all its ideas and to feel through the decoration to the bare structure of the building and the growing lines of the stone. But in an instant I found a catching in my breath, for there was here an echo of terror. Here were the same stresses and strains as in the life-size sculptures but on such a superhuman scale that they seemed to threaten my very existence. It occurred to me, after this, that perhaps in order to understand architecture one needs just as good a head for masses as a mountaineer does for heights. By keeping myself immersed in the safety of personal preoccupations and ideas about, rather than feelings of, the things I was looking at, I suppose I had managed to feel secure on all my past tours round churches; and when in the streets it was easy to be so filled with purposes as to look at buildings with a blind eye. But now that I had realized this terror of thrusting pillars and arches that loomed and brooded over me I found, as always before, the dread of annihilation merging into a deep delight.

After this I slowly came to understand more about the problem of relaxing when amongst other people. Just as I had once found that invisible feelers could be spread round things, so I now found that I could spread them round people as well. But here, more than ever, I needed to have some basis of security before I could do it, for so often I had a feeling that there was something to be guarded against, which time and again came between me and the people I wanted to know. It took me a long time to realize just what this fear was. Although I understood by now well enough that in the world of perception what I wanted was to lose myself in the thing perceived, yet it was too terrifying a thought to be fully admitted when it was a matter of another person. And since I could not recognize it for what it was, it remained at the level of blind thinking and kept me perpetually straining to guard against the very engulfment which I wanted.

In the end the knowledge of my deliverance came

suddenly. Of course I had had many hints and part understandings of what I was trying to escape, but the full realization did not come until one day when I happened to have been looking back over all that I had discovered. I had just begun to ponder over the fact that all the things which I had found to be sources of happiness seemed to depend upon the capacity to relax all straining, to widen my attention beyond the circle of personal interest, and to look detachedly at my own experience. I had just realized that this relaxing and detachment must depend on a fundamental sense of security, and yet that I could apparently never feel safe enough to do it, because there was an urge in me which I had dimly perceived but had never yet been able to face. It was then that the idea occurred to me that until you have, once at least, faced everything you know – the whole universe – with utter giving in, and let all that is 'not you' flow over and engulf you, there can be no lasting sense of security.

Only by being prepared to accept annihilation can one escape from that spiritual 'abiding alone' which is in fact the truly death-like state.

I realized now that as long as you feel insecure you have no real capacity to face other men and women in that skill of communication which more than any other skill requires freedom from tension. By communication I did not of course mean only intellectual conversation but the whole aesthetic of emotional relations; and just as I had, when first beginning to examine my experience, found most of my delights in natural things, I was now finding that I chiefly reckoned each day's catch of happiness in terms of my relationships with others. Of this, wordless understanding seemed to be particularly important. Before, I had been inclined to judge the value of meeting with my friends largely by what was said. Now it was the unvoiced relationship which seemed of more concern – though this was perhaps partly the result of having for eighteen months shared the life of someone who had not yet learned to talk.

Here also I began to discover a new world of direct communication, not through the symbols of words and actions and gestures, but what seemed to be an almost direct interchange of emotion which came with this spreading of invisible feelers. It was not only that my own perceptions were heightened, not only that by spreading myself out towards a person I could 'feel the necessities of their being', it was that they also seemed to receive something, for in no other way could I explain the changes in their behaviour. For instance, I was one day helping a very old lady from her chair to her bed. She was so old that she was past the age of reasonable understanding, and was like a child in most things, including the disinclination to go to bed. She was so heavy that I did not know how to deal with the situation at all and I felt embarrassed, tightly withdrawn, wishing it were over. Then I caught sight of her helplessly obstinate feet and something in them drew me out of myself into her problem, so that it became my problem too, and at once all her obstinacy vanished and she yielded easily to my help. Of course it was quite probable that she detected a subtle change in my clumsy efforts to help her; but there were other times when a person's mood would change when I had made no outward movement whatever, only spread internal feelers. So, when trying to persuade my baby to go to sleep I would often wait beside him, absolutely motionless, but my own heart filled with peace. Once I let impatience and annoyance dominate my mind he would become restless again. This may have been sheer accident, of course, but it happened so many times that in the end I found it very difficult to escape from the belief that my own state of mind did have some direct effect upon him.

Now also communication came to include the whole intricate texture of communal living. Just as I had once learnt to look at colours and shapes for their own sakes, I now began to see, as possible ends in themselves, actions like house-work which had before seemed to be nothing but tiresome routine because they were not 'getting me anywhere'. Now I was beginning to find that part of the day's happiness came while sweeping or preparing food (always before I had hated house-work because after so much time spent there was so little to show for it); I seemed to like it because it was a kind of communication, it expressed my feeling for the house I kept clean and the people who lived in it. Of course I did not always manage to achieve this disinterestedness, just as I could not always see things for their colours and shapes rather than for their use in furthering my private purposes. There were many times when I could not see my actions at all for their own sake, I must sweep from house-proudness because visitors might notice the dirt and think derogatory things, or I must cook a good dinner because that was the sort of person I liked to imagine myself. But I never found that the house-work I did for these reasons appeared in my day's list of happiness.

I now saw too how my earlier discoveries could be applied to this problem of communication. For quite early in my enterprise I had found that to want results for myself, to do things with the expectancy of happiness, was generally fatal, it made the stream of delight dry up at the source. (Of course the greater part of every day was filled with jobs which had to be done in order that

something else might happen; but I am not here dealing
with necessities imposed from without, only with how to
manage one's actions and attitudes where there is any
freedom of choice.) So now I began to find that it was
no way out, as I had once hoped it would be, to want results for other people. In my exasperated self-absorption
I had envied those who were always doing things for
others. But as I grew more observant I began to see that
this by itself was no sure way to peace, for as long as you
expect results from what you do there are here even more
sources of exasperation. Once you assume your right to
interfere in other people's problems they become in some
ways more of a worry than your own, for with your own
you can at least do what you think best, but other people
always show such a persistent tendency to do the wrong
thing. And then it was so fatally easy to think that I knew
what was good for other people; it made me feel
pleasantly superior to think myself in a position to help,
and also it made me feel good, feel that I was piling up
some subtle advantage for myself, becoming a more ad-
mirable character. It took me a long time to learn to
resist the feeling that I *ought* to interfere and try to help
people for their own good. I knew others did it and so
felt I ought to, although I was never too clear about what
were best to be done. And then in addition to the feeling
of ought, there was also the sheer pain of another person's
misery, which of course grew greater, not less, as I learnt
to be more perceiving. Gradually, however, I now came
to understand that it was all right to do things for people
as long as I did it for the sake of doing it, as a gesture of
courtesy, the value being more in the act than in the result. If I sacrificed myself for others, it must be, not because I thought they really needed what I had to give
(for this might be an insult, as if I were implicitly putting

myself above them), but simply as a way of expressing my feelings towards them. Here the giving was enough in itself, it was not a means to an end.

So it was that I gradually came to see what great delights were to be found in those moments of detached seeing when I could recognize another mind and yet want nothing from it. Such communication did not always require contact in time and place, for sometimes from a book or a picture I caught a human meaning to add to my stock of day's delights. I came to be not at all surprised at that tiresome attitude of superiority people seem unable to avoid when they can see meaning in a difficult work of art, although I had often been irritated by it myself, and made to feel very small by people who liked music and pictures I did not understand. For now I was myself realizing a cause for this seeming arrogance, since there were times when for me too a picture or a building or a poem would suddenly come alive. These were times when I would be left so exulting in communication, exulting in the human contact with the artist, that I really did feel in that moment of shared experience a quite new and bigger person; so it was difficult not to strut just a little, for blind thinking almost had a feeling that it had done a bit in the creating of the beautiful thing itself.

CHAPTER XVI

Retrospect

> Whatever it be, whether art or nature, that imprints in us
> the condition of living by reference to others, it does us much
> more harm than good; we deprive ourselves of our own
> utilities, to accommodate appearances to the common
> opinion: we care not so much what our being is, as to us and
> in reality, as what it is to the public observation.
>
> MONTAIGNE

I NOW decided to look back and see what I had achieved in the seven years of this enterprise.

I had set out to try and observe moments of happiness and find out what they depended upon. *But I had discovered that different things made me happy when I looked at my experience from when I did not.* The act of looking was somehow a force in itself which changed my whole being.

When I first began, at the end of each day, to go through what had happened and pick out what seemed best to me, I had had quite unexpected results. Before I began this experiment, when I had drifted through life unquestioningly, I had measured my life in terms of circumstances. I had thought I was happy when I was having what was generally considered 'a good time'. But when I began to try and balance up each day's happiness I had found that there were certain moments which had a special quality of their own, a quality which seemed to be almost independent of what was going on around me, since they occurred sometimes on the most trivial occasions. They stood out because of a feeling of happiness which was far beyond what I had ordinarily meant by 'enjoying myself', and because of this they tended to oust all other concerns in my daily record. Gradually I had come to the conclusion that these were moments when I had by some chance stood aside and looked at my experience, looked with a wide focus, wanting nothing and prepared for anything. The rest of my enterprise had then become an attempt to find out what this ability to look depended upon.

Not only had I found that I enjoyed different things, but I also wanted different things. When I was living blindly I was pulled this way and that by all manner of different wants, but when I stopped to look at them their clamour died down and I became aware of others which seemed to emerge from far deeper down in myself.

I also became aware that happiness in the sense I have described does matter. I was as sure as that I was alive, that happiness not only needs no justification, but that it is also the only final test of whether what I am doing is right for me. Only of course happiness is not the same as pleasure, it includes the pain of losing as well as the pleasure of finding.

My next discovery had been that although I now knew what made me happy I could not achieve it whenever I wanted to. There seemed to be endless obstacles preventing me from living with my eyes open, but as I gradually followed up clue after clue it seemed that the root cause of them all was fear. And I had only been able to discover the origins of this fear by learning a way of observing the habits of my blind thinking. I had found that there was a perpetual self-centred chatter which came between me and my surroundings, and me and myself, and till I had learnt how to silence it I was liable to live in a world of distorted make-believe, cut off from any vital contact between my real needs and my real circumstances. When I could break through it, and only then, was I able to see clearly enough to choose those circumstances under which happiness could grow; to learn, for instance, to limit my activities, not to run after every new thing, not to expend all my energies on the effort to keep up with what other people did just because they did it, so that I had no vitality left for needs that were personal to me.

During my explorations I had also discovered something about science. I had set out by using the scientific method of observation, to find out what made me happy, and then found that it had led me beyond the range of science. For in observing what made me happy I had found something which could not be communicated, something which was an essentially private affair; whilst science, so they say, deals only with 'whatever can be passed from one social being to another'.

I realized then that at one stage I had become disgusted with science for not giving me what was not in its power to give. One warm summer evening, steaming out of London on a week-end train, I caught a glimpse through the window of a fat old woman in apron and rolled sleeves surveying her grimy back garden from the door-step. At once I was seized with an impulse to know more about her, and then began wondering what the scientists who deal with different phases of social life could tell me. I had even got as far as resolving to read some books on sociology, when it suddenly dawned on me that that was not at all what I wanted: I wanted to know that woman as a person, a unique individual, not as a specimen. It was only later, when I read that science is concerned, not with individuals but only with specimens, that I began to realize why I could not find what I wanted in science. For it seemed to be just the unique qualities of particular experiences which I wanted. When I considered anything that happened to me in terms of science, I had to split it up into parts and think only of those qualities which it had in common with others, so it lost that unique quality which it had as a whole, the 'thing-in-itselfness' which had so delighted me in wide perceiving. I wondered whether this was why sometimes, when I came out from reading in a scientific library, the first whiff of hot pavement, the glimpse of a mangy terrier grimed with soot, would make me feel as though I had risen from the dead. For this 'dogness' of the dog and 'stoneness' of the pavement which I loved so, were simply non-existent in abstract 'dog' and abstract 'pavement'. It seemed to me then that science could only *talk* about things and that discussion broke up and killed some essential quality of experience. Science was perhaps a system of charts for finding the way, but no amount of chart-studying would give to inlandsmen the smell of a wind from the sea. So at one time, with the usual 'all-or-noneness' of blind thinking, I had been inclined to repudiate the chart altogether because it was not also the sea.

But if science could not tell me *what* was most important in my experience because importance seemed to depend on unanalysable and incommunicable wholes, I found that it had at least told me something about methods for comparing experiences. For it was science that had shown me that blind thinking, because unable to compare one experience with another, had prevented me from knowing at all what was most important for me and kept me perpetually drifting at the mercy of circumstance. And it was science which had suggested the way to emerge from this blind thinking, by means of expression. But if I had only taken into account those things which science admitted, I would have had to stop short almost at the beginning of my journey.

This does not mean, of course, that science would not have a good deal to say about the material my method brought to light. It was quite clear to me, for instance, that the ideas I was discovering must have wide psycho-analytic implications. The reason why I did not at any time make the attempt to express what I saw in terms of conventional psycho-analytic concepts was that I wanted to keep rigidly within the bounds of my own actual observation, to try as far as possible to forget everything I had read, everything I had been told, and to assume nothing that did not emerge out of my own direct experience. In this way I had thought I might eventually be able to devise a method which might be available for anyone, quite apart from whether opportunity or intellectual capacity inclined them to the task of wading through psycho-analytic literature or their income made it possible for them to submit themselves as a patient. This did not mean that I underestimated the value of psycho-analytic knowledge, small or great, it only meant that I had come to the firm conclusion that reading must come after one had learnt the tricks for observing one's mind, not before; since if it comes before it is only too easy to accept technical concepts intellectually and use them as jargon, not as instruments for the real understanding of experience. As for submitting myself as a patient, I had once managed to do this for several months, a period which would of course be considered only a preliminary stroll by the Freudian school. I cannot tell exactly what happened, but I certainly found it an immensely interesting experience, and it had the concrete result that before I began I had often wished that I were a man, and that after it I never had such a wish again. As this analysis occurred shortly after I had begun the undertaking described in this book, I cannot in fairness omit mention of it; but I do not think it materially affected the development of my method, or that the lack of it would make such a method impossible for anyone else.

However this may be, it is certainly true that, after having developed the technique described here, I did find it possible to make some use of the published psycho-analytic knowledge in interpreting my own material, knowledge which would before have seemed to me far-fetched and unnecessary. And this was the more useful, since the psycho-analysts had always given me the feeling that they considered the unconscious mind as a sort of special preserve which no layman must tamper with. Certainly, since by definition it seemed to be something that you could not possibly see in yourself, there seemed to be no choice but humbly to accept their statements about it. In fact, there was simply nothing you could do. If they told you something about yourself and you agreed, then that seemed proved; but if you denied it, then it was, they said, proved all the more. But as a result of my own experience I was forced to the con-clusion that, by using special methods of observing, I could actually watch some of the ways of the unconscious mind in myself, and, if not reach to the bottom of it, at least extend my consciousness far beyond the ordinary limits of awareness.

The scientific contribution to which I thought I owed most was the study of the ordinary conversation of children.* It was from this that I received the idea of the unconscious mind, not as a dark and gloomy place into which only the psycho-analytic high priests had passports,

*Piaget, op. cit., p. 114.

but as a kind of mental activity which was different from rational thought but none the less an existent reality, observable just as children's conversation can be observed. It was from this that I made the discovery which shed a flood of light on all my problems, the discovery that there was a kind of thinking in myself which in the usual way passed completely unnoticed, and that this shared the characteristics which had been observed of children's thought, it was liable to the same misunderstandings and distortions. Without this idea I doubt whether I should ever have learnt how to develop a technique for studying my own experience.

Certainly one result of my enterprise was clear, I had at least managed to emerge from the state of vague drifting in which I had originally found myself. But what was the crux of my solution, where lay the critical point of my discovery? In these days so much is written deploring the present state of affairs, present morals, present inertia, present ideals; everywhere it is said, 'We must do this, we must do that, must be more courageous, must love our neighbours more, must get rid of lies and hypocrisy.' But hardly anywhere is heard the question, 'What have we the power to do?' Finding that no one offered me an answer, because they had not even asked the question, I had to find one for myself. And I had found there were certain things I could do by effort, but others I could not. I could make myself move but I could not make myself move skilfully, just by saying 'I will'; I could make myself get up and go out to play tennis however lazy I felt, but I could not, simply by saying I would, make myself avoid serving a 'double'. I could, under normal circumstances, force myself to say whatever came into my head, or force myself to say nothing; but I could not by force ensure that what I said

would be interesting. I could, sometimes, force myself by
will to hide an emotion; but I could not by will force
myself to feel one. I could not by direct effort feel love
towards someone, or by direct effort make myself happy.
What then was entirely under the control of my will? It
seemed to me that the only thing that was even potentially so controlled was my attention. I could not control
what I saw when I looked in a certain direction, but I
could, generally at least, control what direction I should
look in. Also it was what I did with my attention,
whether I let it wander unobserved or held it still and
expectant, whether I spread it in feelers beyond my
body or narrowed it to a pin-point of brightness within
my brain, it was this which determined what I saw.

So it was that I had learned something about the
'cans' and 'can'ts' of willing, learnt that it was not any
good willing myself to be more myself, or to live by my
own standards, or to keep my personal integrity and be
sincere with myself. It was no more use than sitting in
the driving seat of a car and willing it to move when you
know nothing of the use of the different levers. So it was
that I had discovered, for instance, that selfishness is not
usually a failure of will, it is not that one deliberately
sees a selfish and an unselfish attitude and chooses the
selfish. It is that one is selfish because one unwittingly
indulges in a kind of thinking which cannot, by its very
nature, recognize the realness of other people's needs.
Clearly, then, sermons exhorting to unselfish action are
useless without an explanation of the meaning of unselfish thought. It seemed that blind thought was selfish
thought, therefore if my thought was blind, if my mind
was full of the kind of thoughts which can never see
beyond themselves, then my actions would also refer to
myself alone, whatever my will and ideals might say.

But if I had learnt how to still the self-centred chatter and let my mind become filled with the being of another, then no willed virtue was necessary.

And the only way to escape from this kind of thinking was again not by willing but by understanding its nature. By continual watching and expression I must learn to observe my thought and maintain a vigilance, not against 'wrong' thoughts, but against refusal to recognize any thought. Further, this introspection meant continual expression, not continual analysis; it meant that I must bring my thoughts and feelings up in their wholeness, not argue about them and try to pretend they were something different from what they were.

I had also learnt how to know what I wanted; to know that this is not a simple matter of momentary decision, but that it needs a rigorous watching and fierce discipline, if the clamouring conflict of likes is to be welded into a single desire. It had taught me that my day-to-day personal 'wants' were really the expression of deep underlying needs, though often the distorted expression because of the confusions of blind thinking. I had learnt that if I kept my thoughts still enough and looked beneath them, then I might sometimes know what was the real need, feel it like a child leaping in the womb, though so remotely that I might easily miss it when over-busy with purposes. Really, then, I had found that there *was* an intuitive sense of how to live. For I had been forced to the conclusion that there was more in the mind than just reason and blind thinking, if only you knew how to look for it; the unconscious part of my mind seemed to be definitely something more than a storehouse for the confusions and shames I dared not face. For was there not also the wisdom which had shaped my body up through the years from a single cell? Certainly this was unconscious, my deliberate will had had no hand in it. And yet I could see no way of escaping the idea that it was mind in some sense; nothing I had ever heard about chemistry made it possible for me to believe that such a job could happen as a result of the chance combining of molecules. Yet if it was my mind in some sense, why should I make a line between mind and body and limit its powers only to ordering the growth of cells? Certainly my exploring had gradually made me aware of the existence of something – I can only call it a wisdom – something that seemed to be 'shaping my ends', trying to express its purposes in pictorial symbols. And it certainly was not a reasonable wisdom, for as soon as I tried to argue and to split up my experience into logical ideas, then this sense of what I wanted was destroyed. To reason was to be actively assertive, and apparently it was only when I was actively passive, and content to wait and watch, that I really knew what I wanted. Though of course once I knew that, then the more good reasoning I could use, to discover how to get what I wanted, the better.

And blind thinking was the enemy of this unconscious wisdom in the sense that it became so muddled between itself and other people that it never knew which was a mere matter of fashion and which the dictates of an inner knowledge. It could, of course, talk glibly about Inner Light and easily give to its egocentric impulses and confused imaginings a false authority. It could make me pretend I was being true to myself when really I was only being true to an infantile fear and confusion of situations; and the more confused it was the more it would call to its aid a sense of conviction. Yet for all its parade there was as much in common between its certainties and the fundamental sense of my own happiness as between the windy flappings of a newspaper in the gutter and the poise of a hovering kestrel. And only by experience of both, by digging down deep enough and watching sincerely enough, could I be sure of recognizing the difference.

*

By keeping a diary of what made me happy I had discovered that happiness came when I was most widely aware. So I had finally come to the conclusion that my task was to become more and more aware, more and more understanding with an understanding that was not at all the same thing as intellectual comprehension. I had come to realize that it was not, after all, a question of a life of consciousness as against a life of natural impulse; for without consciousness, for me at least, there was certainly no freedom of natural expression, but only a clash of haphazardly acquired conventions and a welter of opposing and misunderstood ideals. Without understanding, I was at the mercy of blind habit; with understanding, I could develop my own rules for living and find out which of the conflicting exhortations of a changing civilization was appropriate to my needs. And, by finding that in order to be more and more aware I had to be more and more still, I had not only come to see through my own eyes instead of at second hand, but I had also finally come to discover what was the way of escape from the imprisoning island of my own self-consciousness.

Epilogue

Although I had from the beginning set my face against spending my time in actually looking amongst books for what I wanted, I had, for other reasons, been forced to read fairly widely during these years. It was natural, therefore, that I should keep my eyes open for any clues to my personal problems that might happen to turn up.

Two of such clues I have already indicated. One of them, the discoveries of Piaget about the characteristics of childish thought, had turned out to be so important to me that it had altered the whole course of my observations. The other, Janet's observations of a kind of thinking characteristic in neurosis,* had given me a vivid description of my own difficulties, had provided me with the invaluable word 'chatter' to describe the quality of preoccupations, and had also made me familiar with the idea of varying levels of potency in thinking. But for the rest I had not found very much that seemed directly relevant to my problem. I had of course read a little and listened to much talk of Freud. Clearly the idea of the existence of the 'unconscious mind' had influenced me to expect the unexpected in my explorations; but although my knowledge of Freud's work did to a large extent determine my method I did not find that it helped me much in interpreting what I found. My own discoveries certainly predisposed me to believe that what Freud said about individual development was most likely true. I even fancied I could trace echoes of attitudes he described in my own dim memories, for some of his seemingly wilder statements had a curiously

*Pierre Janet, *Les Névroses*.

familiar ring as if I was just on the verge of remembering such experiences myself. But I did not find that I could apply these explanations to my own particular problems. I thought it was indeed most likely that, for instance, early oral-erotic experience could be discovered which might explain all my worries and fear of difficulty, but I knew also that the theory presupposed these experiences to be buried too deeply in the unconscious part of my mind for me to be able to discover and disentangle them myself. I did not see then that I could make much use of Freudian interpretations to assist my enterprise. Neither did I find much illumination from the various offshoots of the psycho-analytic school. I had, for instance, read something of Jung and tried very hard to determine exactly what was meant by extraversion and introversion. It seemed quite clear that I was an introvert however it was defined, and that my troubles were due to being too much of an introvert, but I could not find out at all why I was one or how to stop being one. Yet for years I felt that this formulation of Jung's was very nearly useful to me, only there was some essential clue missing.

It was not until after I had finished writing this book that I happened one day upon another approach to this same fundamental distinction, one which struck me at once as a most decisive contribution to my problem. In the first place it was a biological approach, and it gave me a definition of the two opposing attitudes in biological terms which seemed to leave no ambiguity. I read:

In this (sexual multiplication), as in many forms of protozoa, we see adopted a mechanism which has proved so satisfactory that it has been continued in all the many-celled plants and animals. The egg cell or female gamete, slow-moving, placid, enduring, receptive, occupies itself with accumulation and storage of food and libido for the ultimate purpose of creation –

in a word, introverted; and the male gamete, active, impetuous, courageously self-sacrificing, with no reserves, resistive in the extreme, bent on forcing its personality and its body substance on the waiting ovum, possessing all those characteristics of the amoeba which are for action upon the outer world – in a word, extraverted.*

Here at least was a concrete picture of the meaning of the words, but I found also that the statement had far-reaching implications. In my earlier struggles with definitions I had heard it maintained that women were typically introverted and men extraverted. This, when I considered all the various descriptions of the respective attitudes, seemed so palpably absurd that I had put out of my head the connexion between the two attitudes and sex differences. But now I read:

Sex equality is no myth, for we are each of us essentially whole.
   It does not matter how deep below a complete surface feminity we have to dig, there we find a complete male striving for expression. It does not matter how far down in the depth of the psyche we have to probe to find the woman in the painfully self-assertive male, there is the other half of the psyche in its entirety seeking for outlet and finding it by many strange paths.†

This seemed to me a promising hypothesis, and since I was now clear enough about my own findings to be no longer afraid of being confused in my search by other people's theories, I decided to find all I could from books and conversation about this fresh approach.

The central idea seemed to be that although in every living being there exist the two aspects, these do not grow at an equal rate, and it is the conflict between these two sides of the personality, and the relation of this to the physical sex, which is at the root of a great amount of psychological difficulty both in children and adults. I

*T. J. Faithfull, *Bisexuality*. J. Bale, Sons & Danielsson Ltd, 1927.
†*Op. cit.*

remembered the drawing I had made (p. 89) in which the chief figure seemed to be faced with two alternatives, the obvious maleness of a sharp-shooter girl on horseback, the no less striking femaleness of the swooningly passive figure on the left. When I first studied this picture it had occurred to me that I could at that time achieve neither of these attitudes, neither the abandon to action nor to passivity. Now I thought that perhaps I might restate the difficulty in terms of bisexuality and say that it was the conflict between my ideas of the male and female attitudes themselves which prevented me from reaching the fullness of either. And to state the problem in these terms did not seem to be a mere matter of terminology, for I suspected that such a restatement carried with it implications that would repay further enquiry. I therefore set out to see whether such a hypothesis was borne out by the rest of my discoveries.

My first thought was that my early discovery about how delight came when I stopped trying may have been a first achievement in the understanding of real femininity. Of course I had realized that these good moments occurred when I was able to wipe out my own identity and let the thing I was looking at take possession of me, and I had eventually come to see this as a first step towards that psychic surrender without which the physical surrender was inevitably incomplete. But I had not before understood that the obsession with purposes which had seemed to keep me from such surrender might be in part the attempt to express an inevitably present maleness. Such an interpretation might also explain why I had not been able to make more use of the mental training systems that offered such glowing rewards in efficiency and success. They were interested only in the development of maleness, of objectivity; and it was perhaps because the unconscious urge that I was blindly trying to express was to do with femaleness, with subjectivity, that I got little help from them and had had to develop my own method. I had certainly discovered that my main purpose was to have no purpose, to learn how to give up effort. Here Lao-Tze, who had given me clues before, could I thought have given me another if only I had known how to interpret it:

He who, being a man, remains a woman, will become a universal channel.

Such an interpretation also shed some light on differences in types of religion. I had at various times found myself considerably attracted towards certain of the Eastern philosophies and had been puzzled at the average Westerner's misunderstanding of them. Now I saw that just as I, although searching to test the depths of the female attitude, had feared it as a spiritual death, so the average Westerner may fear the Eastern glorification of the receptive attitude to life, fear that if he is not perpetually active and efficient everything he knows and clings to will cease to exist.

This interpretation also seemed to explain a striking antithesis which had often puzzled me in people's views of the high point of living. I had read:

It is my fate to utter a secret that has not been uttered for a very long time, namely, that every sort of action is a necessary evil, a teasing, though doubtless inevitable, interruption of the true purpose of life.*

But then I had also read:

Not to be occupied and not to exist amount to the same thing.†

and again:

*J. C. Powys, *In Defence of Sensuality*.
†Voltaire.

the truth of man is in his individuality, not in losing himself in bliss, but in the sharp pain of consciousness.*

Now I could answer, however, why must the truth of man be one-sided at all? Surely it is in his capacity for both that he really exists.

I could see now that I had unknowingly accepted the male assumption that the purpose of life was to have purposes and to get things done. Sometimes I had read criticisms of women's work, usually written by men, maintaining that they should not make the mistake of trying to express themselves in man-made forms but should develop a characteristically feminine approach. This sounded sensible, but apparently I was so imbued with the man-made forms that I was always puzzled about what, in practice, a feminine view-point and style might mean. It was only when I had begun to try and observe my own experience that I had discovered that what I had casually assumed of myself, what I had tried to be and felt I ought to be, was something quite different from what I was – that there was in fact something urging me to a purpose which I did not know. So it was that slowly, at first only in occasional glimpses separated by months or years, I had come to realize that there are two fundamentally opposite ways of approaching experience, both of which are necessary.

The next problem was to interpret the reasons why I myself had been so slow to learn that by relinquishing I could produce riches, so reluctant to understand that:

– to be on a level with the dust of the earth, this is the mysterious virtue.†

or that:

Vessels of moulded earth are useful by reason of their hollowness.

*C. B. Purdom, 'The New Spirit', *New Britain*, 20 September 1933.
†Lao-Tze.

What was the source of this fear of surrender in terms of the bisexuality of the human psyche? Was it that for blind thinking, with its inability to see more than one thing at once, the satisfaction of the female meant the wiping out of the male for ever? To satisfy the desire for surrender to the full without the loss of one's individuality, perhaps this was an idea beyond the powers of blind thinking to grasp, since for it things must be either one or the other. And in its terror of losing the male in the female it had in fact lost both.

I saw now the advantage of calling the two opposing attitudes male and female where I had before only called them active and passive, for it emphasized the fact that each attitude is deeply engrained in, linked with, and growing out of bodily states. If the feminine is unsatisfied physically, then there is a tremendous force urging to the psychically feminine in what seems to be an entirely mental situation. This idea also had considerable bearing on the problem of the uses of the will, it suggested reasons why I so often could not still my anxious purposes by any of my carefully chosen and practised acts of relaxation or standing aside. For the unreasonable fears which could be dispersed by means of expression made up only half of the picture; the form of the fear was certainly determined by the absurdities of blind thinking, but the force behind it came from a real emotional need.

In fact, this whole approach, by emphasizing the natural rhythms of emotional development, made me see this problem of the control of mood as far more a matter of growth than of determination. And one could not make oneself grow, one could only by careful observation find out the conditions of growth and attend to these rather than to the hoped-for results.

As for the question of how an over-receptive attitude,

or its opposite, develops in the first place, I gathered that it was determined by the actual direction of love attitudes towards the child by those most intimately in contact with him. Apparently the natural bias towards maleness or femaleness in a child (which does not necessarily correspond with the sex of his body) can be utterly distorted by the adults around him, by the extent to which they continually draw upon him for love or try to impose their will and personality upon him. A 'spoilt' child, perpetually forced into the position of receiving love, may become so fixed in the receptive attitude that he will continue the female response in situations in after life where it is quite inappropriate. So not only does this inopportune femininity arouse anxiety through the lack of normal physical outlet, but this same anxiety then has an effect upon the person's actual capacity for sensible behaviour.

Next, I tried to see whether using the idea of male and female attitudes, instead of active and passive ones, might not throw some light on the problems I had encountered in trying to learn how to think reflectively. My discovery that in order to relax physically I must first be active mentally seemed to indicate that when I was passive towards my own thought it automatically slipped into contracted effort and tenseness. Now it seemed to me that just as the impulse to be feminine urges one, in relation to other people, to a passive acceptance of their ideas and outlook, so in relation to one's own thought it urges towards a passive suffering of experience rather than an active watching or attempt to express it. So my discovery of a natural rhythm of awareness was perhaps the discovery that reflective thinking requires a subtle balance of male and female activity. Was it not true, or at least useful, to say that as long as I remained all female in my thinking I was passive towards it, leaving it to think itself, unexpressed and unwatched, so that it had all the characteristics I have described for blind thinking, which Piaget called egocentric?

This discovery of the need for a male-female rhythm in my thought, a seeing phase in which I stopped and looked back on the blind phase, seemed to link together most of the different formulations which I had found useful. For instance I read:

Reflexion is discussion carried on inside one.*

Thus I could say that my failure to reflect, my inability to know what I liked or what I wanted, or to draw any conclusions from the welter of my experience, was due to letting my musings remain in the form of an unconscious monologue. I had certainly failed to recognize the truth of Weininger's contention that 'Duality is necessary for observation and comprehension'; I had undoubtedly been quite at sea about how to live my life until I had learnt to make that active gesture of separation and detachment by which one stands aside and looks at one's experience. And it seemed that my reluctance to do this was due partly to the fear of what I might find there, but also to difficulty in allowing the internal male and female to interact.

*Pierre Janet, *Psychologie Expérimentale*, p. 182. MSS of Lectures in British Museum.

Afterword

NEARLY fifty years after I wrote this book I received a letter saying that an American firm was interested in publishing it, something that had not happened before. The letter said, however, that they would like a small addition to it, answering the questions: how did I come to write the book and what impact did its discoveries have on my life and future writing? And so, in 1981, I wrote this Afterword for the American edition. Now, sixty years since the book's beginnings, this British edition is being reprinted.

The first question is easily answered. The book grew out of the fact that when I was 26 (in December 1926), I began to keep a diary. This was because it had slowly become clear that my life was not as it ought to be, although from an external viewpoint it was going very well, since I was earning my living in interesting work, having a full leisure life and plenty of friends. At one stage I thought the trouble might be that my capacity for concentration was deficient so had tried a well-recommended mental training course. However, the first task it demanded was that I should decide what my aim in life was. As I found that I had not any idea about this, I decided to keep a diary and write down what I thought was the best thing that had happened during the day, in the hope that I might find out what it was that I really wanted. I had also been stimulated by reading Montaigne's essays and his insistence that what he calls the soul is totally different from all that one expects it to be, often being the very opposite.

As the book shows, the results of my diary keeping

218

were most surprising, since it turned out that the best things were not at all what one would expect them to be, not to do with successes, either in friendships or work or play, they were mostly very small moments of a total change in the way I was perceiving both the outer world and myself.

As for the second question about the impact on my life and future writings, I suppose it can be said that I was so astonished at what my diary keeping had shown about the power of the unconscious aspects of one's mind, both for good and for ill, that I eventually became a psychoanalyst. As regards my writings, I could say that, with one exception, all subsequent books and articles were concerned with this aspect of human life, either with my own or with my patients'.

When the book was first published, it received many thoughtful, reflective reviews. In the comments of the reviewers, I was able to locate aspects of the work's impact that helped me not to lose sight of my own discoveries, a losing sight that would have been all too easy in the daily demands of parenthood and the need to earn a living. In fact it was the fear that I would do this forgetting that finally made me write the book.

In a review published in *The Listener* (November 1934), W. H. Auden writes of the way I managed, by the fuse of free-association writing and drawing, to catch the wandering thoughts of the moment and put them into words; also how the results were as startling to me as they would be to anyone who chose to apply the method, as startling and as devastating to one's self-conceit and prefixed self-image. He goes on to add: "It would be unfair to her book, which is as exciting as a detective story, to give away all the methods she tried, but they included both physical and mental exercises, the former paralleling in an interesting way the work of Mr Matthias Alexander."

In addition, he said I had discovered that the unconscious is not only the refuge of childish fantasies and fears but also a source of creative wisdom. He adds that my story culminates in a mystical experience.

At that time I knew nothing about the work of Matthias Alexander, though I was to explore it later. As for the term mystical, I was not really prepared to accept that. However, there were one or two other reviewers who also used the term to describe some of the area to which my explorations had led me. For instance, F. W. Laws (*The New Statesman*, December 4, 1936) wrote: "She believes mystically in an 'inner fact' of individual living which escaped identification."

I thought: this "inner fact"—is it really so mystical? Isn't it just the astonishing fact of being alive—but felt from inside not looked at from outside—and relating oneself to whatever it is?

However, another reviewer, (in *The Times Literary Supplement*, unsigned, and with the date torn off the cutting) did not insist on calling the experience "mystical," but simply talked of my descriptions of: "those strange moments of unexpected and inexplicable happiness that are experienced by most sensitive people . . . and the slow recognition of the power of the unconscious in affecting thought and behaviour." I thought; yes, and not just its power in stupid ways, stupid mistakes, but also in ways that showed it knew better than I did where I had to go.

Among the very many letters I received there were a few that made me think that one day I would also have to try and find out more about the relation between mysticism and madness.

Another reviewer, James Young, M.D. (*The New English Weekly*, May 2, 1935) wrote: " . . . the record of her attempt to resolve the struggle between the hard-driven willed rationalism of contemporary academic education (First Class Honours in Psychology) and a truer and more primary perception of reality—not willed under the *duresse* of herd-efficiency . . . is in its way a *tour de force*." Then he quotes from my book, emphasizing the bodily aspects: "Experiencing the present with the whole of my body instead of with the pinpoint of my intellect led to all sorts of new knowledge—and new contentment."

I thought now, of course, this phrase perceiving with my whole body, this is what happened so startlingly that day in the Black Forest. But this reviewer also, like some of the others, commented on my descriptions of the devastating antics of my blind thinking.

There was one reviewer (Olga Martin, *The New Statesman*, 1934) who was particularly interested in what I had experienced about ways of concentrating and the effects of wiping my mind free of thoughts and desires. For instance, she quotes the bit I wrote about how, when looking at a faded cyclamen, I remembered to say to myself: "I want nothing" and at once was totally flooded with colour, "as if I had never before known what colour was." She adds: "Generally this 'flooding-in' happened by chance, but Mrs. Field discovered certain methods of achieving the necessary 'wide attention'." It was also Olga Martin who wrote that I was: "Not content merely to unearth the egotism of childish thinking. In relation to people, as in relation to music and nature, the defenses of spiritual virginity must be broken down. It was not enough, she found, to marry and bear a child; unless one is willing to 'immerse' oneself in the destructive element as Conrad puts it, relationships are apt to be sterile."

I thought now, how little I realized then what a long journey I had set out on and how much forgetting the way to this desirable end there would be.

Someone who signed herself Doris Eastcourt (*The Yorkshire Post*, February 13, 1935) was also interested in the same theme. Under a subheading of "Losing Desire and Finding Joy," she goes on to talk about those early discoveries of mine that increase in depth of perception came with the suspension of effort and desire and thus of the constant interference of the conscious mind. However, she uses the word passivity for that suspension, which I did not think was quite the right word, since I found it usually needed great activity to reach this state. Thus Keats's term "diligent indolence," with emphasis on the "diligence" seemed a better description. This writer also talked of the difficulties of such suspension, using my term "fear of annihilation".

Here I remembered how this kind of diligent suspension had led to discovering new ways of moving, in physical skills, as well as new ways of looking and listening and some of the reviewers referred to this.

The idea I had developed of trying to explore many of my discoveries in terms of an inherent conflict between the male and female aspects of one's psyche turned up in many of the reviews. Thus, Olga Martin also wrote: "If the states of mind of the artist, the mystic and the lover could become available for people who are none of these things, then the cult of power which informs nationalism, capitalism and the rest would have fewer devotees . . . if the bisexual nature of man (admitted by Freud . . .) were generally recognized, then the values appropriate to the suppressed feminine urge would be given their proper place in society and our problems would be tackled in a more peaceful and understanding spirit. Instead of thwarting his hidden femininity Western man might find repose and inspiration in yielding to it."

Stephen Spender (*The Spectator*, 1934) also found the theory of bisexuality interesting, though he felt it was subject to certain objections. Auden, on the other hand, was doubtful whether speaking of male and female elements explains anything. As for me, when I eventually became a psychoanalyst I was to be continually faced with men's fear of their own femininity, if one uses the word in the sense that Hamlet did: "a kind of gain-giving as would perhaps trouble a woman."

Another reviewer made the bisexuality theory central. (Olaf Gleeson, *The New Era*, January 1935): "The path that Mrs Field has chosen is not for everyone. One can see, while reading, the dangers she has encountered and happily, passed . . . Her experiments in free-association demonstrate immediately the validity of the Freudian view-point, though that is now almost *vieux jeu*. It is when she soars freely, with pinions unhampered by previous knowledge, that the real value of the book emerges. . . . She has rediscovered, in her curious pilgrimage the secret of that universal symbol, which lies neither at the base of conscious willing nor even of conscious enjoyment, but at the roots of anthropo- and cosmo-genesis. It is embodied in the *Ankh* and included in the mystery of the Pythagorean Tetractys. It is likewise in the unsuspected meaning of the phrase, 'Male *and* Female created He them.' Whether the author realizes the importance of her discovery it is impossible to say."

I found out afterwards that the Pythagorean Tetractys was said to mean "the marriage of four."

Someone who signed themselves as C. McC. (November 1937 in *Women in Council*) wrote: "It is a practical psychology from a nonprofessional point of view and that's the pity of it." This reviewer also pointed out that I did not advocate the more advanced teachings of yoga and ignored its rules of diet and breathing. Later I was to explore all of these.

Several of the other reviewers also brought in this theme of the difference between Eastern and Western approaches to life. This was to affect my thinking during all the years following 1932, but not to the extent of giving up, or trying to, the Western approach. I was, as always, when any conflict emerged, convinced that I must seek for a marriage between the two protagonists, not an either/or solution.

There was also a review headed *Editorial* in a journal called "Welfare and Personnel Management" (December, 1934) which said: "In an age of 'private lives' very few of us have lives of our own. The lives that provide no copy for the popular film or the best seller, are invaded by the machinery of the economic system. A fundamental problem of our time is to reconquer the territory.

"In her last chapters she tried to formulate the discoveries. . . . The feminine quality of her Eastern thought is foreign to a Western culture shaped by a peculiarly masculine struggle against Nature. That is why the industrial hemisphere needs this thought so much."

Yet another review (*The Daily Herald*, January 3, 1935, and signed "M") ended by saying that although I decided I had suppressed too many of my female tendencies, I did not go on to conclude that I was unhappy because I had a job and a brain and that the woman's place is the home and for a woman to exercise intelligence is to invite trouble.

Also (In *The Morning Post*, December 1934 and signed H.H.) one reviewer, under the heading of "Discovering Balance" quotes something I had said about what I wanted: "not knowledge but to feel the actuality of things; Knowing is no good unless you feel the urgency of the thing. Maybe this is love; your being becomes part of it, giving yourself to it." I thought, yes, feeling the urgency, not imposing one's own on it, is this usefully called female?

It was not until 1962 that I found a published assessment of what I was trying to do by a Professor of Psychology. It was in T. H. Pears's *The Moulding of Modern Man* (Allen & Unwin, 1961). In his book he, like many of the reviewers, emphasizes how I distinguished the two ways of perceiving, the one with narrow focus, seeing life as if with blinkers and from the head, the other this knowing with the whole of one's body. Incidentally, it was here that my attempts to define the way I had been using the terms male and female came in useful, for surely the wide knowing is a containing act, as against a male penetrating one.

About my book as autobiography, since it is concerned, not with external events, but with my reaction to them, Pears says how unfashionable that was, at the time, because behaviourists implied that reports, even of practiced introspectionists, would be dubious because independent validation was impossible. He then tells how: ". . .

J. B. Watson, in his time a valiant anti-introspectionist, once confessed to having, when young, used visual imagery to design apparatus, but possibly thought that about this early mistake the less said the better. . . ."

Pears goes on to add that my series of introspections is more relevant than those in Aldous Huxley's *The Doors of Perception* since most of his references are to mescalin intoxication.* Here I thought: of course, when I wrote *A Life of One's Own* the widespread use of drugs for "psychological trips" was far ahead, including the dangers of "bad trips." In any case, when such use became popular I still preferred to get "there," whatever "there" may be, under my own steam.

There was another aspect of Spender's review that I now find especially relevant. He had called his review "The Road to Happiness," and, when talking about my diary keeping, he said: "She seems always to have had a clear aim before her: the motive was not self-interest: it was happiness: she wanted to discover happiness for herself and happiness for other people in their relation to her. It is important to emphasize this purpose in her diary because criticism can be leveled at the book as an example of psychoanalysis. For any self-analyst is bound to be one-sided. Yet in order to achieve some external aim, a one-sided self-analysis is a legitimate instrument." Here I would have to add that I very soon realized, as in the diary entry for January 7, 1927, that the search for happiness was only half the story; for I remembered Blake's rhyme:

> *Man was made for joy and woe;*
> *And when this we rightly know*
> *Thro' the world we safely go.*

This was certainly to be central in my work with patients, the endeavour to give them a setting in which they could discover the truth of this for themselves.

Marion Milner, 1986

*The Doors of Perception, Chatto & Windus, London, 1954